Human Tuning

John Beaulieu

Published by BioSonic Enterprises, Ltd., High Falls, New York 12440

Cover Design: Phillipe Garnier, Sage Center, Woodstock, NY
Design and production: Pamela Kersage
Editing: J.M. Sirko & Associates, Inc., Lake Katrine, NY
Photographs: Lars Beaulieu

Cymatics Photographs courtesy of MACROmedia

Library of Congress Control Number: 2010924104

Beaulieu, John.
Human Tuning

Bibliography: p.
1. Music therapy   I. Title.   II. Title: Human Tuning

Manufactured in the United States of America

The lessons taught in Human Tuning do not give you legal permission to diagnose, pre-
scribe, treat or engage in sound healing practice for any human illness or condition without
qualifying in your local jurisdiction, obtaining a license or certification, if necessary. Each
state and county has different laws concerning the practice of healing and health provid-
ing. You should consult your local association or attorney before you provide any services.

TABLE OF CONTENTS

———■———

Beginnings

WE ARE SOUND

Imagine that the whole universe, everything we know, including cars, computers, airplanes, houses, buildings, lakes, oceans, continents, our bones, flesh, and nerves is a fountain of dream images generated and sustained by a submerged sound. Further imagine that everything we do and think, whether good or bad, moral or immoral, is an attempt to seek out and merge with that sound. Our goal is to return to the source of the fountain. Although we may identify with the object of value, i.e., a man or woman, a car, etc., the real attraction is the resonance we experience when in the presence of that person or thing. The experience vibrates us like a tuning fork and becomes a sonic homing buoy confirming our inner journey.

Further imagine that you are a being of Sound composed of many tones. Your shape, movements, desires, and motivations, come from an inner concert. Everything you know and feel is Sound. Your concert is everywhere. When you dance, your body organs will make sounds and your muscles will play the correct tones. Your voice will sing praises, and the stars will shine upon you.

The Anechoic Chamber
How I Discovered Human Tuning

discovered that tuning forks could be used to tune the human nervous system in 1974. I was working at Bellevue Psychiatric Hospital in New York City under a research grant from New York University. A psychologist colleague of mine, who knew of my interest in sound, told me about an anechoic chamber located at New York University's psychology laboratory. An anechoic chamber is a scientifically engineered room of complete silence and darkness. I immediately arranged to visit the laboratory in order to experience the anechoic chamber.

I learned about anechoic chambers in John Cage's book *Silence*.[1] John Cage was a New Music composer, philosopher, and author who went on a search for total silence. In his book, *Silence*, he tells of his experiences in an anechoic chamber at Harvard University. Sitting in total silence and darkness, he heard a high and low-pitched sound. Upon leaving the anechoic chamber, the engineer told him the high-pitched sound was his nervous system in operation. The low-pitched sound was his blood in circulation.

The first time I sat in the NYU anechoic chamber, I immediately heard the high-pitched sound of my nervous system and the low tone of my blood circulating. After a few minutes I heard swallowing sounds, stomach growls, mouth pops, heart beats, air entering and exiting my nose and mouth, little clicks in my spinal joints, and even the sound of my eyebrows when I blinked. Over the next two years, I spent over 500 hours sitting in the anechoic chamber listening to the sounds of my body. I tested the effects of different tuning forks as well as mantras and toning, and recorded their effects on my nervous system.

The sound that most interested me in the anechoic chamber was the sound of my nervous system. I observed that the sound of my nervous system was directly related to different physical, mental, and emotional states. For example, if I was calm, my nervous system would make a low, even, soft sound. One day after an argument with a subway attendant, I sat in the anechoic chamber and observed that my nervous system sound was higher pitched, louder, and had a screeching quality.

[1] Cage, John. *Silence*. Middletown, NY: Wesleyan University Press, 1965.

After over 500 hours of listening to my nervous system, I suddenly realized that the nervous system could be tuned like a musical instrument. I went into a music store in Greenwich Village and bought C and A tuning forks, which were the only tuning forks available at the time. When I entered the anechoic chamber once again, I listened to the sound of my nervous system. I tapped the tuning forks on my knees and brought them to my ears. The two sounds instantly merged into one pulse, and I simultaneously noticed two very distinct and yet clearly related changes. I heard the sound of my nervous system change to match the sound of the tuning forks. I then noticed a shift in the way I held my body. I had the distinct experience that my whole body and the sound of my nervous system were one.

I realized then that I needed more tuning forks. It was very difficult to get them in 1973. I was driving to a conference in upstate New York when a state trooper pulled me over for speeding. He saw my two tuning forks on the seat and said, "What are those for?" I blurted out that I was a therapist at Bellevue Psychiatric Hospital and that I was doing research on sound and the nervous system. I think my nervous system must have been very loud at that moment.

To my surprise, the state trooper told me to come into his car and bring my tuning forks. He called in my plates, and then something completely unexpected happened. He showed me his tuning fork. He had a 3000 cycle tuning fork which he used to calibrate his radar gun, the one that caught me speeding. He tapped it and turned a dial on the radar gun until the tuning fork and radar gun came into resonance. He then turned the radar gun so that I could see it and proceeded to tell me exactly how fast each passing car was traveling. He couldn't see the radar gun, and he told me that when he was "tuned in," he just knew the cars speed without looking at his radar gun.

I told him about the anechoic chamber, how I was using tuning forks to tune my nervous system, and that I wanted to get tuning forks made to my specifications for research. He said he would find out who made his tuning forks and get back to me. Two weeks later, he left a phone message with the name and number of the sound lab we use to make our tuning forks to this day. I called them and they made my first set of tuning forks. I had them tune the forks to Pythagorean ratios and a lower fundamental tone then the current musical standard. Just in case you are wondering, the state trooper gave me a speeding ticket. I have never forgotten this experience. An important lesson was learned that day: When working with sound "keep your feet on the ground and your head in the clouds."

The eight tuning forks I ordered in 1974 are exactly the same as the Solar Harmonic Spectrum set we use today (see Solar Harmonic Spectrum Chapter, page 61). My original work in the anechoic chamber was based on systematic experimentation with each Pythagorean interval. This is a form of research called phenomenological research which focuses on the effect of the tuning forks on consciousness. I approached the experience of tuning forks by keeping a journal with specific protocols to help me better understand my experience of the sounds. Each week I would sit in the anechoic chamber and immerse myself in an interval and record my experiences. I would relax, listen to my nervous system, and tune myself to an interval. I realized that each interval was a gateway into different states of awareness complete with thoughts, emotions, and sensations.

Throughout this book I have provided journals to help you systematically experience the tuning forks. It is important to remember that although the science and theory of tuning forks is important, the real teaching is in the experience of the sound. The more you work with the sound the more you will learn. The following story illustrates the importance of experience.

In 2001, I brought my tuning forks into a lab at the State University of New York to test their effects. The biochemists were skeptical and made systematic preparations to measure the tuning forks for days. Within seconds the computer graph showed the release of nitric oxide when we tapped the Otto 128 and vibrated a cellular culture. We did the experiment several times. Once it was clear that the tuning fork caused a nitric oxide spiking reaction, I passed out Otto 128's to each scientist. They immediately began tapping them and putting them on their body to feel the effect. It was an amazing sight to see three scientists in white coats with tuning forks pressed to their heads. At that moment, I went from being called Dr. John to the nick-name of "vibrating John."

The more I worked with tuning forks, the more I understood the sound of my own nervous system. Through this understanding, I began to visually see others as sound. I thought this was unusual until a colleague described a patient as being very high strung. I asked him why he used the term "high strung." He said that the person's body movements were tight like a wound up string, and when he thought about it, he could imagine a high-pitched sound coming from the patient. I realized that hearing a persons sound related to body tone and posture was something we intuitively do everyday. Our language is filled with terms like "high strung," "low keyed," "in tune," "out of tune," and "resonate with" that refer to a person's sound.

Although I experienced the relationship between sound and the nervous system, posture, and consciousness in my experiments in the anechoic chamber, I did not understand how they were related. Today, after thirty five years of clinical practice, research, and experimentation with the tuning forks, I know a lot more. The goal of this book is to share that knowledge so that as you enter into the experience of tuning fork sounds you will have some thoughts, ideas and insights to help guide you. I believe there are many ways to understand the tuning fork sounds. It is my wish that you learn what you can from my original experiences and let the sound guide you into the next level of your journey.

If you want to recreate my anechoic experiences, there are thousands of anechoic chambers in different locations around the world. They are used for all kinds of research from measuring electric noise to measuring the quietness of automobiles. They come in different sizes from a small room to a very large room. You can do a web search for anechoic chambers to learn more about them and their uses. You may even find one and arrange to sit in it. However, it is not necessary because there is another way.

Listening to the Sound of Your Nervous System

To listen to the sound of your nervous system, find a quiet place where you will not be disturbed, sit comfortably, and close your eyes. There should be little to no external sounds. Next, sit quietly, take a few deep breaths and gradually allow your breathing to naturally rise and fall. When you feel relaxed and calm, bring your awareness to the inside of your head or cranium and listen for a high-pitched sound. This is the sound of your nervous system. It sounds similar to the high-pitched background sound of a television but even higher. If you are under a lot of stress, the sound of your nervous system becomes a ringing in your ears. However, most of the time it is in the background, and you just need to relax, clear your mind, and listen to discover it.

The sound of your nervous system is a primary indicator of your current inner tuning. Listen to the sound as you would the sound of a tuning fork. The sound of your nervous system carries a lot of information. Use the following listening suggestions to get inside the sound of your nervous system and perceive its qualities. Feel free to keep a journal based on these listening guidelines.

1. Does your nervous system sound loud, soft, shrill, wavering, pounding, or flowing?

2. Does your nervous system sound have a color? Is it green, yellow, blue, red, etc?

3. Does your nervous system sound have a temperature? Is it cool, hot, warm, or cold?

4. Do you have thoughts when listening to your nervous system sound. Is your nervous system sound saying something?

5. Do you get specific emotions when listening to your nervous system sound? Does your nervous system sound want to communicate feelings?

6. Is your nervous system sound taking you on a journey? Are there images, memories, stories, or visions?

7. Do you hear more then one sound? If so, what is the relationship of the sounds? Are they harmonious or are they dissonant?

8. If you hear more than one sound, listen to each sound separately and follow steps 1 through 7 for each sound. Then follow steps 1 through 7 for the relationship of the sounds.

Once you get to know the sound of your nervous system, it becomes easier to listen to it. For example, you can listen to the sound of your nervous system before you go to sleep, when traveling, after a conversation, or any time you want. When doing this type of listening, do not try to change the sound of your nervous system. Neutrally observe the sound and its qualities in the context of the listening situation.

By doing this, you will come to understand yourself and be able to experience the direct effect of tuning forks. Think of listening to your nervous system as the baseline for evaluating others, exploring different tunings, and opening the gateway into different states of consciousness. Over time, the information, exercises, and protocols presented in this book will help you tune and retune yourself as necessary for both healing and the exciting journey of life through all levels of consciousness.

PART 1

Sound, Healing,
and Energy

PRELUDE

Trash on the street in the form of papers and dried leaves is picked up by a gust of wind and swirled upwards in spirals and loops creating twisting, meandering patterns. Each piece of differently shaped paper, discarded and unimportant, suddenly becomes living, pulsating, and mobile through an invisible merger with floating, dipping, gliding, bending and twisting air. Listen…the spiritual master is everywhere.

Anechoic Reflections

When I sat in the anechoic chamber, I was prepared for the experience of isolation. In 1969, I began practicing yoga and I spent many hours with my eyes closed in quiet environments repeating mantras. I went on silent retreats where I spent ten to fourteen hours a day meditating and doing yoga postures in isolation. The idea of using sound to transcend the mind was very much a part of my meditation training. Through my experiences in the anechoic chamber, I was able to explore many areas of my mind. Each sound was a gateway that took me to different states of awareness which I preferred to call tunings. The mind is like a radio or television, and tuning forks are ways of changing the channel through tuning the nervous system.

When I sat in the anechoic chamber for long periods of time, I became aware of resonances that pulsed within different centers of my brain. I had thought that these centers were like crystal oscillators that conducted specific waves of energy. Through different sounds, I was able to activate and amplify these centers. When I allowed my awareness to merge with the amplified wave, I would often enter alternate realities and dimensions where I communicated with other beings and intelligences.

One day I realized that all the realities and tunings I was exploring were generated from a common energy Source. The Source was greater than my mind and was the "key" that allowed my mind to move effortlessly throughout different experiences, dimensions, and realities. It was then I knew that healing is about the constant adaptation and creativity necessary to tune and retune our nervous system to the Source. I came to understand the modern view of the Source by many names based on the discipline that developed the term. For example, Source in physics is the concept of a zero point field, in systems theory the idea of the supra system, and in set theory the idea of a null set. The term I liked the most was simply the Universal Energy Field.

Sound and Universal Energy

The concept of a Universal Energy Field that connects everything, although unique to the language of science, is not new. Other cultures have discovered it in more intuitive ways and given it different names. The Bible calls the Universal Energy Field "the Word":

"In the beginning was the Word and the
Word was with God and the Word was God"
—Saint John

In Hinduism, the Universal Energy Field is sounded as the sacred mantra "OM." The great spiritual teachers of India said that "OM" resonates with a great cosmic vibration so massive and subtle and all-encompassing that everything seen and unseen is filled with it. The mysterious Hermetic text, *The Kybalion*, states that, "While All is in The ALL, it is equally true that The ALL is in All. To him who truly understands this truth hath come great knowledge."[1]

Today the quest to realize the truth of the Universal Energy Field has been taken up by modern science. Although the scientific language is secular and less intuitive, the essence of Universal Energy Field research continues to support the foundations of sound healing. Just one hundred years ago Albert Einstein proposed that energy was matter and that matter was energy in his famous equation $E = mc^2$. Einstein spent the rest of his career attempting to prove the existence of a field of fields which he called the Universal Energy Field. He regarded matter as being constituted by the regions of space in which the field is extremely intense. He believed that there was no place in physics both for the field and matter because the field was the only reality.

To better understand the scientific concept of a Universal Energy Field, imagine that you are living in the year 1492 and the world is flat. One day you learn that the world is round. It still looks flat and everything you are doing is still based on the belief that the world is flat. Questions like: "How do we know the world is really round?" "What does it mean for me?" would naturally arise.

Flatness is a metaphor for reductionist science. The vast majority of medical scientific research is based on a reductionist model. The best way to explain the

---

[1] Three Initiates. *The Kybalion*. Chicago: The Yogi Publication Society, 1940, p. 95.

reductionist scientific model is to contrast it with systems science, which is the scientific model of roundness. Systems science is the transdisciplinary study of the abstract organization of phenomena based on wholes or fields. The basic assumption of systems science is that the whole or field is always greater than the sum total of its parts. The greatest field in systems science is called the Supra System which is equivalent to the Universal Energy Field.

The following story of the elephant illustrates the differences between reductionist science and systems science.

> A group of reductionist scientists were independently sent to study an elephant. The problem was that the scientists had no idea they were working on an elephant. One scientist was measuring the behavior of the foot. Another scientist was measuring the velocity in which the tail wagged. Another was observing the chemical composition of one toenail, etc. Each scientist was published in separate scientific journals in different disciplines. They had no idea that their work was related because each was in their own specialized area.

Scientists can form a belief and then develop a paradigm based on that belief, then do research on that belief, and come to conclusions that will have measurable outcomes. Simply speaking, when we are in a car looking for directions, we can lay out a flat map and find out where we want to go. When we lay it out flat, the road to our destination looks flat, and we follow it on flat roads, and can find our destination. However, just because we arrive at our destination by using a flat map based on a flat world model, does not prove the world is flat.

This only makes sense to us now because we know the world is round. However, in 1492 flat maps were proof of a flat world endorsed by royalty and this belief was taught for thousands of years. It was very difficult for people to see flatness in the larger picture of roundness. Now we know that flatness functions within the larger paradigm of roundness. We do not see it as unusual because we have had five hundred years to think about it.

Today, Super String physicists theorize that the Universal Energy Field is composed of thousands of microscopic strings. These strings vibrate and create patterns which unify and orchestrate the cosmos. What we perceive as a solid object is actually the result of a vibrating string or tone. If the vibration were to cease, the object would disappear. Albert Einstein carried his violin with him wherever he went and discovered the theory of relativity while playing it.

The concept of a Universal Energy Field orchestrated by vibrating strings is not new. Three thousand years ago the Egyptians portrayed the universe as vibrating strings played by a blind harpist. The blind harpist knows all and sees all through his strings which vibrate the universe into millions of different patterns.

Pythagoras of Samos was a Greek mathematician, philosopher, and musician who lived in 550 B.C. He discovered Pythagorean Geometry and is considered to have recorded the world's first facts in mathematical physics. Pythagoras conceived of the whole universe as a vast musical instrument. He called the vibrating strings of the universe the "Music of the Spheres." He developed a musical scale, called the Pythagorean scale, based on universal harmonies.

This is a painted interior of a white ceramic kylix found in Delphi and dated circa 470 B.C.

Apollo, the Greek God of Music and Healing, plucked the strings of his lyre, tuned to Pythagorean harmonics, sending resonating waves throughout the universe. Apollo lived in Delphi, "the navel of the universe," and his sonic patterns were carried by dolphins to the four corners of the universe.

During the Renaissance, the mathematician and theologian Johannes Kepler visualized the whole universe as the vibrating string of a monochord. A monochord is a musical instrument with only one string. The vibration of the string was analogous to the word of God or the Sound of sounds from which everything arises, including man.

Dr. Randolph Stone, the founder of Polarity Therapy, described the concept of strings orchestrating the universe very elegantly:

"Life is a song. It has its own rhythm of harmony. It is a symphony of all things which exist in major and minor keys of Polarity.

It blends the discords, by opposites, into a harmony which unites the whole into a grand symphony of life. To learn through experience in this life, to appreciate the symphony and lessons of life and to blend with the whole, is the object of our being here."[2]

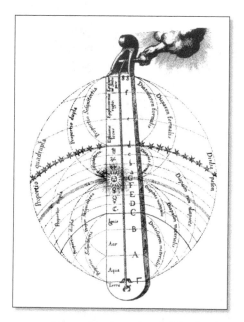

A vibrating Universal Energy Field helps us to understand the insight of musician Sufi Inayat Kahn when he says, "Many say that life entered the human body by the help of music, but the truth is that life itself is music."[3]

The goal of sound healing is that every moment of our life and every action be in harmony with the Universal Energy Field. Abraham Maslow, the founder of humanistic psychology, called the experience of resonance with the Universal Energy Field our "Cognition of Being in the Peak-Experiences."[4] The main qualities of our perception of being one with the larger field were a sense of wholeness and interconnectedness which people experienced as perfection, completion, effortlessness, playfulness, simplicity, aliveness, and a profound sense of truth and well-being.

We all know and have experienced these words. They describe our essence and our inner wellness. The name given by Eastern mystics for these words is enlightenment. The word mystic comes from the Greek *myein* which means to close your eyes and use your sense of listening. All of us are enlightened all the time. It is just a matter of listening, remembering, and allowing the larger field to flow through our whole self as we perform our daily activities. The result is a unity between the polarities of our internal and external environments which creates a resonance with a potential infinite wellness.

---

[2] Dr. Randolph Stone. *Polarity Therapy: The Complete Works. Vol I. Polarity Therapy & Its Triune Function*. Reno, NV: CRCS Publications, 1987, p. 5.

[3] Sufi Inayat Kahn. *Music*. p. 79.

[4] Dr. Abraham Maslow. *Toward a Psychology of Being*. New York, NY: Van Nostrand Reinhold Company, 1968, p. 71.

Universal Energy Visualization

Imagine being on the beach on a warm day looking at the ocean. Your eyes gradually move from the ripples of the tide bubbling and moving in all directions, to the waves swelling and breaking, to the horizon where the ocean meets the sky. Here the whole ocean appears to gently rise and fall in a very slow pulse. Be with the slow pulse of the ocean and feel it in your body.

Next, notice how the rolling waves are connected to and rise from the slow ocean pulse. Follow them as they move toward the shore. Watch their rhythms change as they cross each other, bob up and down, and their speed appears to increase. Suddenly they rise up and break, creating the audible sound of the ocean which is seen coming to shore as hundreds of thousands of tide rhythms within rhythms.

Sound and Energy Field Healing

There are energy fields within energy fields which are all created and sustained by the Universal Energy Field. If an energy field, small or large, loses resonance with the Universal Energy Field, it will lose energy and eventually cease to exist. Conversely, the greater the resonance of an energy field with the Universal Energy Field, the higher the level of energy flowing through that field.

Everything is made of emptiness and form is condensed emptiness.

— Albert Einstein

Regardless of the size of an energy field, it is ultimately generated by energy from the Universal Energy Field. Therefore, the nature of an energy field is to attract energy through resonance with larger fields which in turn resonate with larger fields to eventually resonate with the Universal Energy Field. Like a plant growing towards the Sun, we will do whatever it takes to come into resonance with the Universal Energy Field. In other words, all behaviors, no matter how functional or dysfunctional they may appear, are attempts to come into resonance with the Universal Energy Field.

A fundamental principle of sound healing is that physical, emotional, and mental symptoms are being generated by an underlying energy field. Thus, if we change the energy field, then the physical, emotional, and mental behavior patterns will also change.

A way of understanding the healing ability of energy fields is to look at the effects of different environments. Imagine you are living in an energy field called an urban environment. Everyday you suffer from a runny nose and watery eyes, and you take many different remedies to get through the day. One day you decide to take a vacation and go to the desert. After the first week of desert living, you notice that your lungs are clear and you can breathe through your nose without taking remedies. After the second week, you notice that you are thinking differently and that your emotional responses to situations have changed.

When we are in one environment and we look at the customs of people living in another environment, we sometimes think they are strange. However, if we live in their environment for awhile, we change and come into resonance with the lifestyle produced by that field. For example, people in cold climates wear heavy winter coats. Understanding and buying the right winter coat is very important, and people spend lots of time talking about different winter coats. They get on an airplane bound for the Caribbean, and when they get off the plane, their winter coats come off as well. If they were to live for any length of time in the Caribbean, their winter coats would be thrown away and their conversations would switch to swim suits.

I began to think about the dynamics of energy field shifting while working with patients with multiple personality disorders. I worked with a woman with eleven documented personalities. Over a period of several years I learned each personality and her anchors for shifting between personalities. One personality would come to my office with a cold, and when she shifted into another personality, the cold would disappear. We see similar shifts with patients who have cancer who go into remission. One day they have cancer, and the next day it is gone. From a energy perspective, remission can take place instantly based on a field shift. When the new field emerges, endogenous biochemical cascades that destroy cancer cells appear naturally as part of the new field.

Scientifically, an energy field is defined as a medium that connects two or more points in space through energy expressed as tone or vibration. It is a challenge to understand energy field dynamics. This is because energy fields are normally invisible, and we tend to notice their effects rather than the tone that created them. Dr. Hans Jenny of Basel, Switzerland developed Cymatics to help us intuitively understand energy fields and their dynamics.

Dr. Jenny performed his Cymatic experiments by putting substances such as sand, fluid, and powder on a metal plate. The plate was then attached to an oscillator which is a device that produces vibrations. The oscillator is controlled by a frequency generator which causes the oscillator to vibrate the substances on the plate at different frequencies.

Imagine any popular electronic massage vibrator or go to most any department store and ask to see their massagers. Turn it on and it will vibrate or oscillate. Next, place the massager on a bone. Feel how the vibrations are amplified over your body. Touching the massager to your bone is like Dr. Jenny attaching his oscillator to a metal plate. The plate, like your bones, amplifies the vibrations created by the oscillator.

A simple massage device creates only one vibration which can be heard as a hum. The hum you hear with your ears and the vibration you feel from the massager are the same frequency. In contrast to a massage vibrator, which is capable of only one vibration or sound, Dr. Jenny's oscillator was hooked to a frequency generator is capable of thousands of different vibrations or sounds.

When Dr. Jenny turned the dial of the frequency generator, he could instantly change the vibrations moving through the plate. He could observe in real time the effects of different vibrations on different substances. When Dr. Jenny watched the sand or other substances on the metal plate organize into different patterns, he could also hear the sound produced by the oscillator. If he were to lightly touch the plate, he could feel the vibration in his fingertips.

The high speed photographs on the next page taken by Dr. Jenny are of sand and water being vibrated at different frequencies. If you were in the room with Dr. Jenny, you would see the geometric pattern form on the plate and simultaneously hear the tone. If you placed your hand on the plate, you would feel it vibrating. When viewing the photographs, remember that the geometric patterns, which appear solid, are actually created by different tones. The sand and water are actually pulsating on the plate.

In his laboratory, Dr. Jenny observed three fundamental principles at work in the vibratory field on the plate. He wrote, "Since the various aspects of these phenomena are due to vibration, we are confronted with a spectrum which reveals a patterned, figurative formation at one pole and a kinetic-dynamic process at the other, the whole being generated and sustained by its essential periodicity."[5]

Dr. Jenny is saying that one can hear the sound as a wave; he calls this the pole of kinetic-dynamic process. One can see the geometric pattern the sound

---

[5] Jenny, Hans. *Cymatics*. Basel, Switzerland: Basilius Presse, 1974, p. 1.

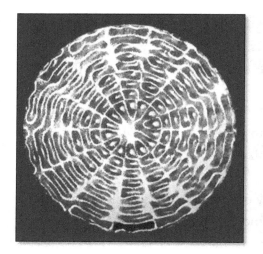
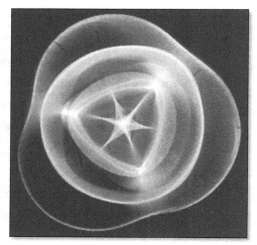

Courtesy of
Jeff Volk Macromedia

creates on the plate; he calls this the pole "patterned-figurative formation." If Dr. Jenny were to touch the plate and feel the plate vibrating, he would call this the generating pole of "essential periodicity."

All three poles—wave, pulse, and form—interact to create a whole field. One cannot have form without wave and pulse or wave without form and pulse. For example, if you tried to change the geometric pattern with your hand, the sand would return to exactly the same pattern. In other words, the geometric pattern, even though it appears to be solid, is part of a whole field which is generated and sustained by an underlying tone or vibration.

One of the most interesting dynamics of a cymatics experiment is the area on the vibrating plate that does not move called nodes. Intuition says that if the whole plate is vibrating, then every area on the plate must be vibrating. However, this is not so. The word node is a scientific term which means "a point at which the amplitude of vibration of a standing wave system is zero."

If you were to closely observe a cymatics experiment, you would see the sand always moving towards places of zero movement within the vibrational field of the plate. It is as though the sand comes to rest for a moment and then jumps back into the vibrational field. The further the sand moves away from the nodal points, the less congruent it is with the lines of the geometric pattern. In systems science, nodes are called attractors. An attractor is a region within an oscillating field that pulls everything towards it. It is an attractor that allows us to shift from one energy field to another.

In the healing arts, attractors are called still points. The key to shifting from one mental/physical pattern to another is still point. Dr. Milton Erickson, M.D., was an expert in using hypnosis and trance states for healing. He called the state of trance "neutral" which is another term for still point. He believed that for a person to change, they must first go into a trance. The practitioner could then guide them into a new life pattern using suggestions.

Once a system enters still point, a change in pattern involves reorganizing around a new tone. In hypnosis, the practitioner offers the new pattern through verbal suggestions. In tuning fork work, the new pattern is introduced through the audible tone of the tuning forks. In hypnosis, the practitioner uses different verbal methods to induce a still point. In tuning fork work, the tuning forks are tuned to naturally induce a still point.

Once still point is induced and a new tone is presented, the change from an old pattern to the new one always involves chaos. For an energy field to change into a new energy field, the original energy field must disorganize and fall apart. When the new tone is introduced, the geometric pattern becomes visually disorganized and chaotic before it transforms into a new geometric pattern.

The scientific term for disorganizing and falling apart is chaos. Chaos has two definitions. The first definition defines chaos as "utter confusion or disorder, wholly without organization or order."[6] This definition describes the experience of chaos in our lives. Everything may seem to be going well when all of a sudden we are thrown a curve ball and our life gets out of sync. We describe these days with popular sayings like "going against the grain," "pain in the ass," "bad hair day," "discombobulated," "crazy," or "I got up on the wrong side of the bed."

Chaos is defined in the second definition as "the infinity of space or formless matter supposed to have preceded the existence of the ordered universe."[7] From this perspective, chaos is a natural part of growth and evolution. It is a necessary part of a continuum of energy fields falling apart and reforming into new energy fields leading to the Universal Energy Field. Learning, growth, healing, and higher states of consciousness are not possible without chaos.

The Nobel prize winning chemist, Dr. Ilya Prigogine, discovered the importance of chaos in shifting energy fields while investigating thermodynamic systems. He found that all living systems dissipate more and more energy over time, causing dissonances within the system. As time passes, these dissonances increase in intensity causing the system to move further and further from equilibrium. Soon everything begins to wobble. The wobbling increases until all preexisting order within the system shatters, causing the system to leap into chaos.

When we make a real change, everything changes. When we experience chaos in our life, it means that something is trying to change. The more we resist the chaos, the more it is like trying to shift gears without going into neutral. In fact, we sometimes call it "the grind" when life is not changing in the way we want. Ideally, making life changes would be as easy as shifting gears on a car. When we recognize a new tone/pattern entering our life, we would naturally go to neutral and allow the new tone/pattern to emerge. When we are driving and first gear is

---

[6] *Webster's New College Dictionary.* New York: Houghton Mifflin Company, 1986, p. 187.
[7] Ibid., p. 187.

ending, we sense the need to change and push in the clutch and shift into a new gear. It can be that simple, or we can grind away.

Tuning forks are effortless ways of empowering change in our life. Their tones are archetypical ideas which spiral around a still point. When we hear them, we are drawn into a still point, and our nervous system naturally shifts into a new tone. The chaos of shifting into a new tone sometimes appears as an uncomfortable feeling, pressure, or need to change how we are standing or sitting. Then it is gone. Most of the time we just shift without even noticing the chaos because our awareness is focused on the new tone.

Sound and the Five Elements

The Universal Energy Field, much like a string dividing to create different tones, divides into five energy fields or elements called Ether, Air, Fire, Water, and Earth. On a cosmic scale, each element symbolizes a universal principle or archetype. The five elements combine and mix in different ways, like musical tones, to generate currents of energy that sustain everything we know and experience including our thoughts, emotions, and physical body. The ancient seers of India called the five elements Shabda or the Sacred Sound Currents. Dr. Randolph Stone, the founder of Polarity Therapy, visualized the points of the five star pattern as "element tones" which sound in varying intensities to create the music of life. He called the five star pattern "Natures Geometric Keyboard."[8]

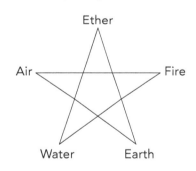

The existence of archetypal elements is recognized in the philosophical, religious, and healing traditions of many cultures. All speak of one primary energy that divides and steps down in currents of elemental energy. Dr. Vansant Lad describes this process of division from an Ayruvedic Medicine perspective:

> *The rishies perceived that in the beginning, the world existed in an unman-*
> *ifested state of consciousness. From that state of unified consciousness, the*

---

[8] Dr. Randolph Stone. *Polarity Therapy: The Complete Works. Vol I. The Wireless Anatomy of Man.* Reno, NV: CRCS Publications, 1987, p. 17.

subtle vibrations of the cosmic soundless sound aum manifested. From that vibration there first appeared the Ether element. This ethereal element then began to move: its subtle movements create the Air, which is Ether in action. The movement of Ether produced friction, and through friction heat was generated. Particles of heat energy combined to form intense light and from this light the Fire element manifested.

Thus, Ether manifested into Air, and it was the same Ether that further manifested into Fire. Through the heat of the Fire, certain ethereal elements dissolved and liquified, manifesting the Water element, and then solidified to form the molecules of Earth. In this Way, Ether manifested into the four elements of Air, Fire, Water, and Earth.[9]

The elements were also known in Western traditions. Greek philosophy was based on a doctrine of the elements. Man's four facilities: moral (Fire), aesthetic and soul (Water), intellectual (Air), and physical (Earth) were seen as expressions of the elements. Hippocrates, the father of Western medicine, based his healing on the four moods, or humours. He termed them phlegmatic (Earth), choleric (Water), sanguine (Fire), and melancholic (Air). The elements were rediscovered in the Middle Ages and the Renaissance by three distinguished scholars concerned with the "music of the spheres." They were the Jesuit Father, Athansasius Kircher, the English Rosicrucian Robert Fludd, and the astronomer, Johannes Kepler. Robert Fludd's World Monochord illustrates the relationship of the elements to sound and creation.

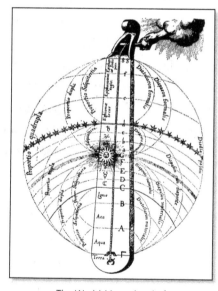

The World-Monochord of Robert de Fluctibus, from his *Metaphysica, physica arque technica...Historia,* 1519

Fritz Stege explains the World Monochord in Music, Magic, Mystery.

The single-stringed measuring instrument with whose aid Pythagoreans worked out the intervals is anchored to Earth (Terra). The latter corresponds to the gamma Graecum, the bottom note of the medieval note-

---

[9] Dr. Vasant Lad. *Ayruveda: The Science of Self-Healing.* Santa Fe: Lotus Press, 1984, p. 21.

system. Above it lies at intervals of a second the other elements Aqua,
Aer, Ignis, (Water, Air, Fire) and thus in fact the whole material world.[10]

The following chart shows ourselves in relationship to the elements.

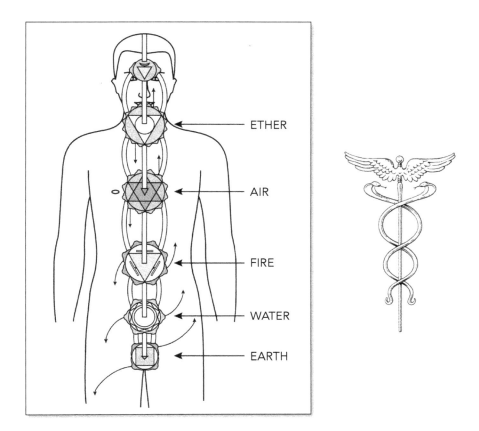

At the center of the chart are the three primary energy currents. These are
illustrated as the ultrasonic core in the middle with two intertwined lines. Together
they form the symbol of the caduceus. The caduceus, or the Staff of Hermes, was
the insignia of the ancient physicians of Egypt and Greece.

Dr. Stone, the founder of Polarity Therapy, explains the meaning of the caduceus symbol:

> *The two serpents represent the Mind Principle in dual aspect. The fiery*
> *breath of the Sun is the positive pole as the vital energy of the right*
> *side of the body. It was called "Yang" by the Chinese, and "Piggala" by*

---

[10] Peter Michael Hamel. *Through Music to the Self.* Wiltshire, England: Compton Press, 1976, p. 94.

the Hindus. On the left side of the body flows the cooling energy of the Moon essence of Nature. This was call "Yin" by the Chinese, and the "ida" current in India.[11]

Although the caduceus remains the physicians' symbol, its true energy meaning is not recognized by those practicing medicine today. The currents of the caduceus can be visualized as waves of energy that divide to create element centers or chakras. The term "chakra" comes from the Sanskrit word which means "spinning wheel of energy." The chakras are symbolized in the diagram on the previous page by lotus flowers with decreasing numbers of petals depicting a step down in vibration. In ancient drawings, the chakras were pictured as spinning wheels without symbolic embellishment.

Balancing the Five Elements

There is no set formula for balancing the elements in a person. Element balancing is a mobile, ever-changing interaction of elements between the self, the external environment, and the cosmos. There is only our ability to participate with each element at the appropriate time. We get sick when element flexibility is lost. The image of a hang glider soaring through the sky is a good metaphor for understanding our relationship with the five elements. The hang glider pilot may appear to be effortlessly soaring; however, on closer examination, he is making thousands of adjustments in response to changing wind currents. The hang glider pilot is paying attention to the wind currents because he knows that if he does not adjust he will crash. When the currents change, the hang glider pilot goes on alert and immediately makes the correct adaptation. We see this as effortless soaring; however, for the pilot, "effortlessness" requires a lot of knowledge, dedicated training, practice, conditioning, and the right mindset to be able to glide effortlessly.

Ideal element balance is obtained by our constant adaptation to the five elements. An element scale can help us better understand the relationship between the five element combinations and adaptation. Each element is assigned a minimum to maximum range of intensity from 1 to 10. Level 1 is the least intense, and level 10 is the most intense expression of an element. Our actions in normal reality

[11] Dr. Randolph Stone, *Polarity Therapy: The Complete Works. Vol I. Energy.* Reno, NV: CRCS Publications, 1987, p. 17.

must match the elemental currents which are generating the event. For example, going to the bank requires an element pattern of 8 Earth, 4 Water, 3 Fire, and 1 Air. Making a point with the Bank officer requires a change to 6 Earth, 3 Water, 7 Fire and 2 Air. Thanking the bank officer requires another change to 3 Earth, 5 Water, 4 Fire, and 2 Air. And driving home requires 2 Earth, 1 Water, 9 Fire, and 7 Air.

Sometimes our actions do not align with the flow of the five elements. There is a Samurai movie in which the main character is a warrior who commands his men at +10 Fire. His voice is loud and staccato. He barks successful fiery military commands on the battlefield, and he is highly respected by his men. Next, the movie shifts from a battlefield scene to his bamboo house where he is lying on a rice mat with his Geisha wife. They are playfully looking into each others eyes. Water is +8 and rising. Suddenly he speaks to her in a totally inappropriate +10 Fire battlefield voice as though he is still commanding his men. She lowers her head and simultaneously a flower wilts as all the water is evaporated by the excess Fire.

The five elements are integral to both Western and Eastern healing traditions, and the need to adapt to changing life situations is very much a part of modern science. Dr. Hans Selye, who won the Nobel Prize, defines stress as adaptation to change. When we fail to adapt to a life change, we create increasing levels of distress in our lives. Those that adapt to change will experience the same stress as euphoric stress or what scientists term U-stress.

Imagine the hang glider soaring through the sky. The wind changes suddenly, and the flyer fails to adjust. An alarm immediately goes off in his body called the biochemistry of stress. He can ignore the alarm; however, the alarm reaction will continue to escalate. It is like setting an alarm clock and trying not to listen to it in the morning. The Samurai warrior was in U-stress on the battlefield, something that might be distress for many, and in distress in the bedroom. It might seem funny; however, the Samurai, from a five element perspective, is an example of someone who needs to learn more about Water element adaptation skills.

Modern scientific stress theory and the five elements theory are very similar. Both emphasize the importance of adaptation to change, and both have therapeutic approaches that help us adapt. In many instances, these approaches are one and the same. The difference lies only in the theory. Stress theory is based on reductionist science and life changes. For example, a therapist may ask you if you have recently lost a family member, changed jobs, bought a house, or gone on vacation. He then assigns a number value to the energy it takes to adapt to each life change. The higher your score the greater your stress level.

The five element theory is more aligned with a systems science approach and focuses on energy fields creating the dynamics of life events. Both systems and reductionist approaches require the ability to observe and evaluate life events and associated behaviors; however, the five element approach requires an additional step of translating life events and behaviors into element patterns. Once the element pattern is understood, it becomes a basis for choosing methods to adapt to different energy patterns as well as a resource to prepare for future changes.

For the purposes of learning, each element is explored by itself; however, they are always present in our lives in different combinations. Methods of evaluating and combining elements in order to create sessions are presented in the chapter on Pythagorean Tuning Forks and The Five Elements. The following element protocols are designed to bring out the qualities of each element for training purposes. They will help you make and hear the sounds of the tuning forks associated with each element. Reading about the element and practicing the protocol is great preparation for creating more complex element sessions. It is suggested that you visualize the color and "feeling tone" of the element before doing the protocol. The protocols can be done with knee taps or overtone taps.

Ether Element

ETHER TUNING FORK PROTOCOL	C–C512 C–G C–C512
KEY WORDS	vision, space
COLOR	blue
EMOTION	(–) grief, loss, remorse, anguish (+) ecstasy, bliss, joy, happiness
TISSUE QUALITY	(–) flaccid, limp, dull, loose (+) elongation, relaxed, soft but firm, resilient/springy
PROFILE	(–) suffering loss, being lost: wondering without direction (+) having a vision, great sense of well-being; balance; space to make things happen; everything is just right; celebration; higher messages
MOVEMENT	open

DISCUSSION

Ether is space. There are many different qualities of Ether in our lives represented by many different types of spaces. Each space has its own dimensions where different activities take place. The activities within the Ether space are the four elements, Air, Fire, Water, and Earth, which are constantly mixing in different combinations. Sometimes we even call these activities "mixers." We can create spaces

for many different types of mixing. For example, we can create internal emotional spaces for happiness, sadness, anger, grief, joy, and peace. We can also create mental spaces for our thoughts. Sometimes we say, "I just need some space to think this over" or "Will you just give me some space?"

We seek out different spaces at different times in our lives. Sometimes we may feel the need for outdoor spaces, indoor spaces, open spaces or enclosed spaces, big spaces or small spaces. We may seek a warm space or cold space, a light or dark space, or different colored spaces. Sometimes we may need a quiet peaceful space, or we may be attracted to a noisy, active, or chaotic space.

New Yorkers are always talking about their living spaces. When I first arrived in New York City in 1973 from Indiana, I looked for a space to live in. I looked at a small New York apartment and felt like I was going to suffocate. When I finally got out of the building, I started taking deep breaths. The real estate agent told me that people from my part of the country need more space. She took me to downtown Manhattan and showed me loft spaces. I found one—it was not pretty, but it was big. In those days, to my surprise, no one wanted to live in a big space. All I knew was that I could breathe freely and feel relaxed in that open space.

When I invited some of the hospital staff to my loft for a party, they had many different reactions to being in my space. One nurse told me, "This space is too big. It scares me. Don't you get lost in here?" A psychiatrist told me, "I have never been in a space like this. My patients would freak out in here." My Music Therapy colleague, who grew up in Texas, understood my need for space. He let out a big holler and said, "Yes! This space is great!"

Space is everywhere in our lives. There are spaces within spaces. We are in the space of our room which is in the space of our house. Our house is in the space of our property, and our property is in the space of our town. Our town is in the space of our county, and our county is in the space of our state which is in the space of our country. Our country is in the space of our world which is in the space of our solar system which is in the space of our universe and so on and so on.

We are always changing and shifting spaces. It seems sometimes we are on an endless search for the right space. When we are tired of being in the space of our room, we walk into another space in our house. We change our external space and then change our internal space. When we enter another room, our thoughts, emotions, and body shift. Writers are always looking for the perfect space to write. Painters need a space with the right light to paint. Cowboys sing about wide open spaces.

Changing spaces is a form of tuning ourselves. This is perhaps the reason why the Ether element is associated with sound. When I was recording at Nevesa Studios in Woodstock we were in a soundproof room. The microphones were turned up all the way in order to record the subtle overtones of the tuning forks. When we listened to the recording, we could still hear a sound that was not coming from the tuning forks. I asked the engineer what the humming sound was in the background. He told me it was the sound of the space of the recording room. He then told me that different recording rooms have different tones.

Spaces within our own bodies are governed by the Ether Element. When the space between the joints of our body is too constricted or flaccid, a dissonance is created within our harmonic field. This causes a change in our thoughts, emotions, and physical body. For example, a compromised space between the joint of our first finger or an articulation in our cranium can have an effect on the energy throughout our entire body.

By understanding and working with Ether, we can become aware of the importance of space in our life. For example, we can be stressed out and take a vacation to the Caribbean. We can leave the small space of our office and enter the open space of a beach. By working with Ether, we can take actions that change our space in order to create a harmonic shift of the wave patterns of the other four elements.

Air Element

AIR TUNING FORK PROTOCOL	C–G C–C512 C–F C–G
KEY WORDS	Thought and Intellect
EMOTION	(–) bargaining, lust (+) compassion
TISSUE QUALITY	(–) fast erratic movement, flighty (+) buoyant, fast movement shifting directions, light, floating
PROFILE	(–) clear thinking, setting goals, excels at problem solving, easy to talk with, giving of self freely, abundance of ideas, and uplifting or light way of being. (+) confusion, scattered, inability to make up one's mind, saying one thing and doing another, talking in circles, impatient, and judgmental.
MOVEMENT	light, fast, quick, darting,

DISCUSSION

Air is everywhere. When we come into this world, the first thing we do is take a breath of air. Wherever we go, we need air. We breathe air even when we are flying in airplanes. We swim underwater and breathe air from a scuba tank, and we breathe air when we sleep. Everywhere we are, we need air

to sustain our life. There are many different qualities of air. We can have fresh and stale air, cold and hot air, humid and dry air, ocean, mountain, and city air. Air can be expansive, buoyant, and fast moving in currents which we call breezes, winds, airstreams, whirlwinds, gales, cyclones, gusts, and drafts.

If someone floats around without any sense of reality, we say they are an airy person. We call someone who is always off in their thoughts an "air-head."

Air is about intellect and thought processes. The Air element loves to move freely and can be uncomfortable or trapped when it slows down. Air in a balloon appears to be stable but is really under a lot of pressure. When the balloon pops the air explodes and escapes. People with a lot of Air element qualities sometimes appear calm yet inside they may be having a lot of thoughts and putting a lot of pressure on themselves. When a person has hundreds of ideas and never seems to act on them, we say that person is airy, an "air-head," or has his head in the clouds. When we do not like what someone says, we sometimes say, "Oh that's just a lot of hot air."

The Air movement pattern is one of speed and zigzag movements in different directions. We sometimes tell children who move like this that they have "ants in their pants." When adults are experiencing the Air element, they may have difficulty making up their minds or making decisions. They may pace the floor, fidget, and quickly move from one room to another. When a group of people have a lot of Air, we say they are "restless." When that Air is contained and directed, we say they are "focused and alert."

When one talks with a person who exhibits an Air voice pattern, they talk fast and sometimes erratically, and switch from one topic to another. For example, a person may say in a very quick way, "I think we should go to the movies, but maybe we should stay home. Or, it might be better just to take a walk. Or, maybe we can take a quick walk, go to the movies and then come back home. Instead of a walk, let's eat and then go to the movies. Or maybe we should eat at home and watch a movie on television." As they speak, their body may move in a fast rhythm and become more and more agitated.

AIR ELEMENT INFOMERCIAL

Air infomercials tell you that you can do it all. You name it; you can do it. These are the travel commercials that let you know you can travel to Hawaii and stop off in Utah for some skiing. In Hawaii you can visit a volcano, go to the beach, play golf, eat at great restaurants, and enjoy evening entertainment in three places. Plus, you can hike, take a helicopter ride, sail, snorkel, and surf. In the end, the announcer explains the ticket and its restrictions faster than any human being can talk. The restrictions, which are Earth, are not that important because you have already done it all in your Air element fantasy.

Fire Element

FIRE TUNING FORK PROTOCOL	C–G C–E C–A
KEY WORDS	movement/motivation
EMOTION	(–) anger, rage (+) forgiveness/motivation
TISSUE QUALITY	(–) shaking, excess heat, friction, feeling of rubbing against (+) vibrancy, warm, feeling of glowing
PROFILE	(–) can't get way, aggression, always wanting to break through or get their way, pushing, overbearing, lots of drama (+) taking action, ready to go, warmth, speaking up for oneself and ideals, movement with direction, forgiving, lots of drama as excitement

DISCUSSION

Fire is motivation. Fire shoots upwards and does this without thinking. The Nike commercial which says, "Just do it" captures the essence of Fire energy. There are many different kinds and qualities of fire. We can have a soft glowing ember fire or a raging fire in our fireplace. The question is always "What kind and quality of Fire do we need?" The answer lies in our imagination and

experience of different fires. Perhaps to sleep well we need a soft warm glowing ember fire. For exercise, we may need a strong bright leaping fire. To motivate ourselves to paint or write we need a spark of fire to ignite our creativity.

When we get really angry with someone, we say, "that person just burns me up." When we really want something, someone may say, "She is all fired up about that." When we are not motivated to do something, sometimes we say, "My fire is low today." When we need to make a change at work and let someone go, we "fire them." In the aggression of war we get "fired upon" and soldiers have "fire power."

When we use up all of our fire, we "burn out." Our body temperature is ideally a steady fire in our body. A high fever is like a raging fire, and a lower more normal temperature is a lack of fire. When we meet someone who really inspires us and gets things done, we say, "He is really a fiery person." Or, if someone does too much and does not know how to stop, we say "He has too much fire."

We were having a Fire day in our Polarity class in upstate New York. The class was in the studio doing fire sessions and making Fire sounds. Outside, about 75 yards from the classroom, I had built a huge bonfire for that evening. I really got carried away and stacked wood above my head. I then got a Fire thought. It just came, and I didn't even question it even though I knew better.

I went to the garage and got the lawn mower gasoline can and I put gasoline on the wood. I thought I had put just a little on to get the fire going. I stood back a good ways and threw a match into the huge wood pile. The next thing I knew there was the sound of a huge "woomph." I was knocked backwards three feet. The windows in the studio pulsed with the shockwave. The students, who were in the middle of their Fire bodywork sessions, jumped up. When they looked out the window, they saw a huge bonfire. Everyone was into the Fire element, and it all seemed as it should be. I picked myself up off the ground with the thought, "You should have known better after all these years of working with Fire. You should not have let yourself get carried away like that."

FIRE ELEMENT INFOMERCIAL

Fitness trainers with mesomorphic (Fire) bodies sell exercise programs and equipment with raging fire energy. They are motivators who inspire us with excited words telling us to go!, go!, go! They tell slow Earth people and bogged down Water people to add fire to their lives. Listen to them and you can pump iron, run, climb mountains, and eat super food. You can do it all "right now"!

Water Element

WATER TUNING FORK PROTOCOL	C – G C – D C – B
KEY WORDS	bonding, creativity
EMOTION	(–) nurturing, loving, caring, (+) jealousy, possessiveness, envy, attachment
TISSUE QUALITY	(–) fluid, flowing, liquid, movement (+) swelling, puffy, spongy, mushy, cold
PROFILE	(–) creative, lets people/things come and go, effortlessness, ease of interaction, loyalty (+) holding on to something/somebody, jealous, possessive, can turn cold, giving the cold shoulder, covert

DISCUSSION

Water flows in many different ways. Water can be a gently meandering stream or a raging flood. Water can gush, spurt, and surge. We can pour water and spill water. Water makes waves, spouts, ripples, whirlpools, currents, undertows, breakers, swells, eddies, and pools.

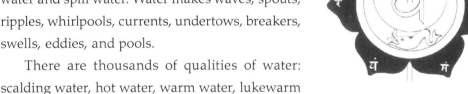

There are thousands of qualities of water: scalding water, hot water, warm water, lukewarm water, cold water, freezing water, and bubbly water. There are bodies of water such as ponds, streams, rivers, creeks, oceans, gulfs, seas, inlets, and reservoirs.

Water is fun. We swim in water, make drinks out of water, enjoy cool mists of water on a hot day, and play all sorts of water sports. We ice skate and ski on frozen water, and we inhale the steam of hot water in steam baths. Water is also dangerous. Water can drown us. Lifeguards learn that it only takes enough water to cover the nose and mouth to drown. Water can also sweep us away, and the rise and fall of ocean water can make us seasick.

Water is necessary for life. Ponce de Leon spent years looking for the Fountain of Youth, and to this day people all over the world seek the healing waters of springs. Without water we would just dry up. When someone is out of ideas or can't continue an activity, they sometimes say, "I am all dried up."

Water is also about flow and creativity. When we are doing a project and the work just happens, we say that "we are in the flow." Water will flow anywhere unless it has boundaries. When a person babbles on and on without any ability to stop, we say that they are "watery." Here is an example:

"I really like Mark because Mark is a good person. He brings me my groceries from the store and he never over-charges. I can always trust Mark to show up on time. I am sure Mark is smart and I know that he is a good boy..."

Then you try to stop them and say, "But Mark is not going to be here tomorrow; he quit!" The conversation continues flowing as though you were a rock in a stream, "Oh, well, I am sure he has his reasons. He is such a good boy and I know he delivered my groceries on time and I am sure he will go on to something else. I wonder what he will be doing next..."

WATER ELEMENT INFOMERCIAL

Water element infomercials always bring us closer, create bonds, and give us a special flow in our lives. Soft music is always a big water element seller. We see images of a couple holding hands, walking along the beach and listening to "romantic classics." The sex and intimacy commercials show us a happy man holding his satisfied wife's hand and telling us the wonders of Viagra. There is a Water commercial made specifically for investors showing a burned out broker (too much Fire) who learns about a "video aquarium" (Water). He watches his video fish swimming, and enters a Water state where he can relax and experience new ideas and hopes for his life.

Earth Element

EARTH TUNING FORK PROTOCOL	C128 Hum with Otto Tuning Fork
KEY WORDS	grounded and centered
EMOTION	(–) fear, terror, possessive, boredom
	(+) security, confidence, patience
ENERGY/ TISSUE QUALITY	(–) contracted, held, hard, pulled in, cold
	(+) strong, solid, firm
PROFILE	(–) afraid to let go, bottled up, holding back, walled off from feelings or part of life, strong belief system and thought patterns, right and wrong tendencies, feeling of not wanting to be too close, enforce, distance via an earth wall
	(+) clear position, straight forward way of relating, gets facts straight, ability to organize information, immense sense of security and trust, feeling of safety with the person, clear boundaries

DISCUSSION

Earth is our mother and the ground we stand on. When we die, our bodies return to Mother Earth and our spirits rise up to our Father in heaven. There are many qualities of earth. We can experience solid earth, hard earth, soft earth, mushy earth, hot earth, cold earth, frozen earth, cracked earth, brittle earth, dry earth, parched earth, moist earth, muddy earth, and fertile earth. Farmers look at the earth, touch

the earth, smell the earth, and feel the earth to determine the right planting time. Earth creates many things; mountains, hills, caves, canyons, valleys, yards, trails, rocks, boulders, stones, stream beds, lake and pond bottoms, and ocean floors.

Earth is fun. We run and jump on earth. Children play in dirt and slide down mud hills. We make mud pies and pottery with earth. We build clay houses and some people live in underground houses. We climb earth, throw earth, and skip stones across water. We move earth with excavators and little boys watch with wide eyes. We plant our gardens in good earth, and spend hours with our hoes and shovels making everything just right with our green thumbs.

When we need to be organized and focused, we turn to earth to "get our feet on the ground." When we are scattered, we are told "to get our act together," which is another way of saying get organized. When we need to be clear about what we are doing, we "ground ourselves." When we meet someone who speaks clearly and usually with a slow and low voice, we say, "that person is really grounded" or "that person really has their act together."

I love to listen to good radio show hosts who help you solve your problems. My favorite host was a man named Dr. Bernard Meltzner who had a radio show in New York City for many years. He would come on the air and say in a low resonant slow clear voice, "Hello, this is Dr. Bernard Meltzner. Think of me as your Uncle Bernard. Lets talk about your problems and solve them." The moment I heard his deep earthy voice I felt a deep sense of security. It was as though whatever problems I might be experiencing would just melt into the earth. I think people tuned into Dr. Meltzner just to hear his voice and whatever he talked about was secondary.

One day, an hysterical woman talking in a very fast air voice called the show. She just went on and on. Suddenly Dr. Meltzner spoke up and said in his deep voice, "Stop. Slow down dear. We will handle this." I couldn't believe the switch in the woman's voice as she replied in a clear and slowed down tone, "Really?" Dr. Meltzner in all his earthly confidence said, "Of course!"

Earth gives us our boundaries and security. In medieval times, castles were built from stones and were called fortresses. When there was a threat, everyone retreated inside the solid stone castle walls for safety. During World War II, people built bunkers deep underground to protect themselves from the bombs. Today, Switzerland and other countries have hollowed out whole mountains for people to retreat into in case of a nuclear attack.

EARTH ELEMENT INFOMERCIAL

Earth infomercials present disorganized people (too much Air) who become organized (Earth) by using their product. They show day organizers to manage your time, kitchen organizers, file organizers, basement organizers. These infomercials begin with crazy, disorganized Air element people who discover the product and instantly become well-organized. My favorites are the financial management infomercials that show a perfectly dressed older man (Earth) speaking with a deep/slow Earth voice asking you to let his company manage (organize) your money.

FIVE ELEMENT JOURNEY
INTERLUDE

BEFORE THE BEGINNING   *Imagine that before you came into being, there existed a potential that floated in a pulsating, undulating, ocean of universal energy. The potential was unbounded, free, and expanded effortlessly in all directions and in all dimensions. One day the potential, like a chick hatching from an egg, or a butterfly emerging from a cocoon, or a young Parsifal leaving the dark forest, realized that it was time to take a cosmic journey. Instantly, the potential manifests as "you," and you are conceived as a being. The journey begins.*

ETHER   *As you begin your journey towards Earth your free spirit begins to manifest in space as a form. You were potential, now you are something. For the first time you begin to experience the beginnings of boundaries. You have no idea what a boundary is, yet you know that your space is defined. You experience your first emotion—Grief. You have lost the pureness of your potential, and your grief is so intense that it is impossible to sustain. You want to go back, and there is no going back.*

AIR   *You are breathing the cosmos and discover the element of Air. For the first time you feel the emotion of desire. You desire your Spirit back and for everything to be as it was before. The search begins for your spirit, and you look everywhere as quickly and as fast as you can. The desire intensifies, and you continue to look and look in every direction.*

FIRE   *The looking becomes frantic. It creates friction, and you enter the element of Fire. The heat builds and builds with the powerful and consuming frustration of not finding your potential. You are burning, and for the first time you feel the emotion of anger. The Fire and anger intensifies until it becomes a primal scream: I want my Spirit back!*

WATER   *The energy expands, and there is a sense of relief as it seems you have returned to your potential. Then without warning, it contracts again, and you enter the element of Water. The intense heat of your Fire has melted the ethereal substance contained within the Air and transformed it into Water.*

Everything begins to cool down, and the element of Water begins to take on a shape of an image of your lost Spirit. Instantly, you feel the emotion of attachment. You are in love with the image you have created, and like Narcissus looking at her image reflected in water, you are in a trance.

EARTH   You cannot let go of your image and lose your spirit again. Automatically, you feel the emotion of fear, and you constrict in order to hold on to your image. Your fear pulls your image together and gives it a solid shape. Your image is real and you are experiencing the Earth element.

Ideal Nervous System Tuning Body Tuners™ [12]

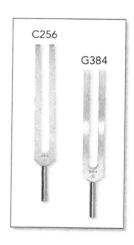

C256

G384

The Perfect Fifth, C and G, is the interval of ideal nervous system tuning. The Perfect Fifth brings all parts of our self into a unified harmony. We intuitively know we are "in tune" because we are one hundred percent involved and simultaneously relaxed and everything seems to go our way. We describe the experience of being in and out of tune in many ways. For example, when someone has a high-pitched nervous system we say they are high-strung, wound-up, or uptight. When someone has a low-pitched nervous system, we say they are low-keyed or wound-down. Words like winding up and winding down are very similar to words used by musicians when they raise or lower the pitch of a string.

The ideal nervous system pitch, a place where there is just the right amount of tension, is called "being in tune." Athletes and performers describe being in tune as an experience of profound inner relaxation that happens when they are

---

[12] I named the Perfect Fifth Body Tuners based on my experiences in the anechoic chamber. When I discovered the effect of the Perfect Fifth I noticed my nervous system and body posture shift into resonance with the sound. I realized that ideal tuning involves both the nervous system and the vestibular system which relates to how we posture ourselves in the world.

competing or performing to their utmost ability. People watching their performance often refer to them as "highly tuned" or "in the zone."

The "perfect" in Perfect Fifth refers to the harmonious sound which unifies opposites. The Chinese philosopher, Lao Tzu, referred to the Perfect Fifth as the sound of universal harmony between the forces of Yin and Yang. In India, the Perfect Fifth is believed to create a sound through which Shiva, the masculine principle, calls Shakti, the feminine principle, to the dance of life. The Alchemists called the Perfect Fifth ("crux ansata") and considered it to be a transition point where matter crossed over into spirit. The "crux ansata" is also called the "anak" by the Egyptians who thought of it as a still point where the earth ends and our ascension into spirit begins. For them, the number five was the perfect combination of even (2) and odd (3) representing the unity of spirit and earth.

The concept of ratio is an important key to understanding the harmonics of the Perfect Fifth and nervous system tuning. A ratio is a comparison of two numbers that represent a relationship between values. A ratio is presented in two ways. The first way is a number followed by a slash and another number, i.e., $2/3$. The second way is to just say 2 to 3. The ratio between sounds can be determined through several methods. The modern method is to measure sounds in cycles per second (cps) for example C is 256 cps and G is 384 cps: $256/384$ reduces to a ratio of two to three $(2/3)$.

In ancient times, they did not have the ability to measure the cycles per second of a sound. To determine its ratio, Pythagoras used an instrument called a monochord. The monochord consisted of a sound box with a single string stretched over a moveable bridge. The position of the bridge is determined by a number scale marked on the side of the sound box. The resulting tonal relationships are based on the position of the bridge, and the ratios are determined by the number scale.

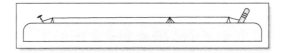

A very simple version of a monochord can be made by stretching a rubber band or string between two nails. You can also use a single string of a guitar or any stringed instrument as a monochord. The string can be any length, thickness, or tension as long as it sounds when plucked.

Pluck the string of the monochord and listen to its sound. The sound of the string vibrating as a whole without any division is called the fundamental. The fundamental sound represents the number 1 because it is the sound of one string.

Next, take a ruler and measure the whole string and then divide it in half. If the whole string is six inches then press the string down at the halfway or three inch point. Pluck the strings on either side of the half point. Adjust their sound by ear until they sound exactly the same; this is the exact half point of the string. The halfway point related to the whole sound of the string creates a ratio of one to two (½) which is an octave. In terms of visual harmonics, one can see with the monochord that the length of the octave string is 3 inches. The length of the whole string is 6 inches; ³⁄₆ then reduces to a ratio of one to two (½).

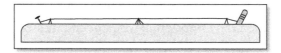

Next, divide the monochord string into three equal parts of 2 inches each. Press the string down at one-third the string's total length.

The sound of the string at the one third point creates the ratio of two to three (⅔) or a Perfect Fifth. In terms of visual harmonics, one can see the length of the Perfect Fifth string is 2 inches and the length of the octave string is 3 inches which is a ratio of two to three (⅔).

The diagram at right shows a caliper calculated to a ⅔ ratio. The large line and small line, regardless of the opening of the caliper, are always in a two to three (⅔) ratio. The center leg of the calipers represents the "point" where the two lines of the caliper merge. It is like the slash (/) which defines a ratio.

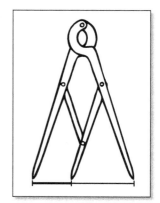

This point of merger can be presented as an empty circle connecting two lines.

The reason for this graphic representation is that the point of merger is a still point connecting the two lines via a neutral field of energy. In sound theory this point would be called a "node" which means a place of zero vibration. A zero point acts like a flexible hinge allowing for movement in multiple directions and dimensions. In the following pictures, the long and short lines are connected by an open point which represents the "stillness" within the sound.

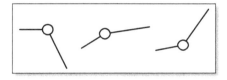

The following diagram shows how the joints of the body are connected in ⅔ rations. Each joint can be imagined as a still point which allows the ⅔ wave to rise and fall through the entire body.

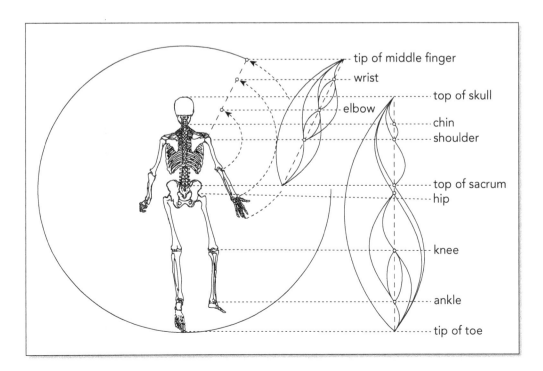

When the autonomic nervous system is tuned to a Perfect Fifth, a ⅔ wave flows through our whole body. The nervous system entrains to the signal and further signals the tendons, muscles, and ligaments connecting each joint to come into a balanced tone. In order for our body to conduct the ⅔ wave, a precise balance of ligamental tension is necessary at each joint. Any imbalance of tension will set up an interference pattern that compromises range of motion.

The key to physiologically understanding how human tuning works is suggested by T. S. Elliot in his poem *Four Quartets* when he says,

> *"at the still point, there the dance is…*
> *neither arrest nor movement…"* [13]

The words "neither arrest nor movement" can be physiologically understood as either the parasympathetic or sympathetic nervous system. The sympathetic nervous system is the "fight or flight nervous system" which has to do with alertness, expenditure of energy, being on the go, and getting things done. The parasympathetic nervous system is the relaxation nervous system which has to do with calming down, conservation of energy, and receiving.

The two nervous systems combine to form the autonomic nervous system. A functioning autonomic nervous system is a constant interplay and balance between the sympathetic and parasympathetic. To accomplish a shift in sympathetic/parasympathetic balance, which will either raise or lower the pitch of the nervous system, the central nervous system (which controls sensory input) must disengage and enter a still point. During a still point, the central nervous system is still functioning; however, the engagement of the autonomic nervous system with incoming sensory information is suspended.

Dr. William Guner Sutherland, D.O., the founder of Cranial Osteopathy, used the term "idling" to describe a non-engaged central nervous system. The term came from his observations of automobiles idling in neutral. For a car to shift gears, the driver must disengage the power to the wheels by pressing down on the clutch (still point). Although the engine continues to run, it is in neutral and disengaged from the power train. In a similar way, a person can be in still point and the autonomic nervous system can continue to fire. They may even "rev up," but they will not go anywhere because they are disengaged from activity.

---

[13] T. S. Elliot. "Burnt Norton." *Four Quartets,* Section II.

From neutral, a driver can upshift, which would be analogous to raising nervous system pitch through more sympathetic activity, or he can downshift, which would be analogous to lowering nervous system pitch through more parasympathetic activity. When the person comes out of still point, their power or life energy is reengaged within a new sympathetic/parasympathetic balance. The tuning of their nervous system then changes to come into resonance with the Perfect Fifth.

Because we are disengaged in still point, we do not notice the shift in nervous system tuning until we reengage. If we shift into a new nervous system tuning that is familiar, than the shift is perceived as "normal." If we shift into a nervous system tuning that is unfamiliar, we may experience some degree of chaos. This is because we are perceiving central nervous system input in a new way and have to adapt to a new set of thoughts, emotions, and sensations.

Within stillness, the human energy system can reorganize and shift into resonance with the Perfect Fifth signal. Dr. John Upledger describes a therapeutic still point from a craniosacral perspective. "The total craniosacral system motion will… become perfectly still… During still point, everything relaxes… Any muscle tension seems to melt away… The still point may last a few seconds to a few minutes. When it is over, the craniosacral system will resume its motion, usually with a better symmetry and larger amplitude."[14]

The Perfect Fifth, from an energy perspective, is a sonic beacon that resonates with the primordial wave of the universal energy field leading to the heart of stillness. When we return to the primordial wave of a Perfect Fifth, we are "in tune."

Perfect Fifth Evaluation

A skilled practitioner can use the ideal of Perfect Fifth tuning to evaluate the state of the human nervous system. A key to Perfect Fifth evaluation

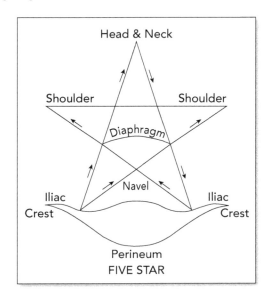

---

[14] Dr. John Upleddger. *Craniosacral Therapy.* Seattle: Eastland Press, 1983, p. 25.

is understanding five star geometry and its relationship to the Perfect Fifth and body posture. The visual geometry of the five pointed star overlayed on the body is a method to evaluate nervous system tuning in relationship to the Perfect Fifth, life energy flow, and universal field resonance. The top of the star is the head. The shoulders are the two top side points, and the hips are the bottom two points of the star. When the relationships between head, shoulders, and hips are aligned to the five star pattern, the nervous system is tuned to a Perfect Fifth and in resonance with the Universal Energy Field.

The graphics below show the Perfect Fifth calipers placed on the pentagram. The points connecting the large and small lines within the pentagram are still points represented as open circles. In human beings, the still points act as hinges that allow the five star to be flexible and move in multiple directions and dimensions via different nervous system tunings. The movements of the pentagram via still points are resonant with the different intervals of the Pythagorean scale.

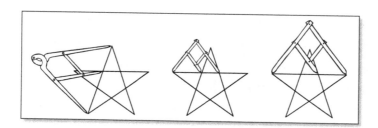

Although the pentagram may be a geometric solid to mathematicians, it is a living, pulsating, dynamic, and adaptable form to sound therapists. In order to resonate with the energies of the elements, the joints in the human body which control five star alignment must be toned and flexible. One way to visualize the five star and its movements is to watch a good athlete perform. The ideal athletic body at rest is in five star proportion, and we say that he is highly tuned. When the athlete is in competition, his body is flexible, pliable, and able to move in many different directions in order to meet the challenges of his opponent.

The Perfect Fifth is like the A tone used to tune a piano. When our nervous system is in tune with the Perfect Fifth, we can move into other intervals and return to the interval of a Perfect Fifth. This changing of intervals can be seen as visual changes within the five star pattern related to the whole body. Each interval and body position is in resonance with the Perfect Fifth, even though the tonal and visual harmonic patterns may be changing.

All of the points of the star are connected through the center of the pentagram within the star. If another star is drawn within this pentagram and then another within the new inner pentagram, then a star within a star within a star appears. This is another geometric representation of a spiral leading to a still point. When we are in tune, there are energy fields within energy fields emanating as waves within waves from the Universal Energy Field.

Leonardo DaVinci's drawing, Squaring the Circle, illustrates the principle of different human tunings through five star visual geometry. The Circle represents the Universal Energy Field, and the square represents Earth. The distance between the Universal Energy Field and Earth is the interval of an octave. The octave creates a space that spans "from above to below." The man stands between heaven and earth. If his shoulders are in balance, he is able to "square the circle" and is in perfect balance. This is the ideal five star pattern and the interval of a Perfect Fifth expressed in human form.

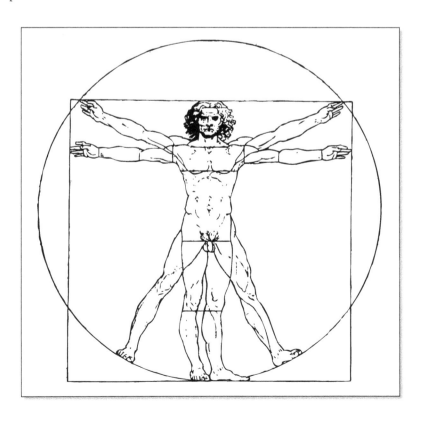

Dr. D. D. Palmer, the founder of Chiropractic Medicine, believed that quality Chiropractic care was based on good nervous system tone. He said that "Consciousness is determined by and must accord with acoustic vibrations."[15] To this day, many Chiropractors determine what D. D. Palmer called proper acoustic tone by observing long and short leg alignment. When the leg lengths measured by comparing ankles are even, it is an indicator of correct tone. If the leg lengths are uneven it is an indicator of being out of alignment with the five star pattern and creates a dissonant tone. The chiropractor performs a spinal adjustment and observes leg length. If the adjustment is successful, the leg lengths will be even, thus creating proper five star alignment and optimal tone.

Five Star Evaluation Process

Several methods can be used to evaluate five star harmonics. In order for these evaluation methods to work, it is important to know your nervous system by working with the Perfect Fifth and other Pythagorean intervals. It is suggested that you read about the intervals in the Solar Harmonic Spectrum chapter and work with them using the Sound Journal in Appendix A.

Dr. Wilhelm Reich energetically pictured the evaluation and healing process as two spiral energy system merging. He called it cosmic superimposition.[2]

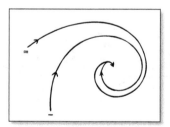

It is only through merging with the energy field of the patient that the healer can truly know the patient. However, knowing the patient also means that the healer has to know him or herself on a very deep level. When one merges with the energy field of the patient, it is easy to lose oneself. Psychotherapists call this "counter transference." It means that something in the other reminds you of something in yourself that is not completely known. The result is that the healer cannot get a clear evaluation of the other.

---

[2] Dr. D. D. Palmer. *The Chiropractor.* Health Research Mokelumne CA, 1970, p. 8.

Knowing the ideal five star is a baseline for being able to observe areas that are out of alignment and their relationship to the whole. For this reason it is very important to work with the intervals and get to know yourself "inside" the intervals. Then, when you evaluate the other, you know the ideal five star, know your relationship to that ideal, and are able to better perceive the other's energy in contrast to your energy and the ideal five star energy.

BASELINE :: Evaluation Exercise 1

Stand up and allow your head, shoulders and hips to move into five star alignment. A mirror can be used to check; however, the best check is to close your eyes and feel the position of your neck, shoulders, and hips in relationship to the pentagram. If a shoulder feels too high, take a deep breath and focus on the tension in the shoulder. Try to relax it just enough to bring it into proper alignment. If an area is too loose, tense it just enough to bring it into the proper alignment.

Next, knee tap the C and G tuning forks on your knees and hum until your voice comes into resonance with the Perfect Fifth. Then stop humming and maintain the felt feeling of the tone. Internally scan your body to get a sense of your overall tension. Then focus on the relationship of your shoulders to your neck. Get both a visual and felt sense of your neck rising up and away from your shoulder creating a space between them that resonates with the tone of the Perfect Fifth.

Knowing the tone of the Perfect Fifth in your mind and body is the baseline for five star evaluation. Do the above exercise many times until you can recognize when you are out of alignment and out of tune. To get back in tune, sound the tuning forks, hum, or think the Perfect Fifth and allow your body to come back into the correct five star alignment. The more you know five star resonance, the better you will be able to evaluate yourself and others.

DISSONANCE :: Evaluation Exercise 2

Tighten your shoulders and allow them to rise up to your ears. Tune into the new tension and hum until your voice comes into resonance with it. As you become tighter, your humming pitch will naturally rise. It is similar to a string. The greater the tension the higher the pitch.

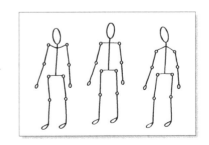

Allow your shoulders to slightly go up and down. Hum and both listen and feel for any constrictions, tightness, or holding in the sound. Listen to the sound and feel the muscle tone around your throat. It is possible to have the shoulders higher or lower and hum a pitch that is open and resonant. However, if the pitch is constricted and/or too open, then the five star pattern is compromised.

The "body knowing" of the feeling and voice tone of the Perfect Fifth is the key to evaluating visual harmonics and hearing the tone of another. Observe the relationship of another's shoulders and neck. Allow yourself to tune into and get the feeling tone for the quality of tension that holds the relationship in place. Tune into the feeling tone of the Perfect Fifth in your body and then allow your shoulders to move into the position and tension of the others. Hum out loud or hum inwardly the feeling tone of the new shoulder position.

When you are in tune with the new tonal quality, ask the following based on a comparison with the Perfect Fifth tone:

- Is the pitch higher or lower?
- Is the pitch tighter or looser?
- What color is the pitch?
- What temperature is the pitch?
- Are there any images that come with the pitch?
- Are there any thoughts that come with the pitch?

To refine your evaluation, visually observe the precise relationship of the shoulders and neck. For example, is one shoulder higher or pulled more forward? Is the tension in one shoulder different than the tension in the other shoulder? Is the neck more forward or tilted to one side? Observe as many details as possible and internalize those details in your body by taking on the position of the pitch and tension.

Next, you can expand your evaluation to the whole five star pattern. Observe the relationship of the hips to the shoulders based on the five star diagonals. Observe the relationship of the neck and head to the hips based on the five star diagonals. Notice any twists, constrictions, and pulls. Simultaneously, allow your body to take on the body position complete with the pitch and tension of the diagonals.

When you finish the evaluation of the five star pattern on someone, you will hear and feel the effect of their tone resonating through your body. The tone is a wave that carries information. Tune into the tone. Hum the tone out loud. Observe what is revealed by the tone, and ask evaluation questions. Quality evaluation is a matter of knowing what you value, i.e., the tone of the Perfect Fifth; its visual harmonics; and the observing, tuning in and listening to what is present in yourself as well as somebody else.

REFLEXOLOGY EVALUATION :: Evaluation Exercise 3

Dissonance within the Five Star tonal system can be mapped to different areas of the body through reflex points. Sonic and visual energy observation can be used to trace the five star diagonals and identify the reflex points that need attention. The following diagram shows the reflex points along the five star diagonals.

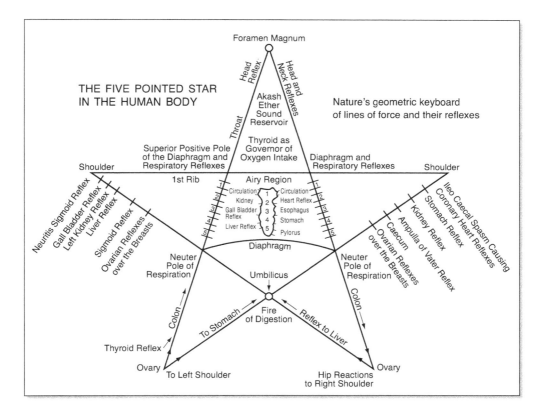

Imagine the diagonals of the five star as strings stretched between pegs. When the strings are the ideal tension, the shoulders, hips, and head will be aligned to the five star pattern. When a string is too tight, it will pull on the head, shoulders, and hips causing them to rotate and/or lift into a compensation position. If a string is too loose, the body will droop or sag without tone.

To visually evaluate the five star pattern, observe the attachment points of the diagonals, i.e., shoulder and hip, head and hip. Note their relationship, i.e., left shoulder is high and right hip is rotated forward. Simultaneously observe the diagonal between them to get a sense of its tension in your body. Hum the pitch of the tension and feel the constriction and/or openness of your sound. Ask yourself, "Is it too tight (high-pitched) or too loose (low-pitched)?"

Next, hum the Perfect Fifth. If it is not appropriate to hum out loud, then hum it mentally. Mark your visual position/point on the diagonal at the places where your voice wavers, constricts, or drops in pitch. Compare this position to the reflex point along the diagonal.

Another method is to tap the Perfect Fifth tuning forks or the Body Tuners. Holding the C256 on the bottom and the G384 on the top, move them along the diagonals. Listen to the overtone sounds. Note when an overtone sound drops out or there is a change, i.e., a waver in the tone of the Perfect Fifth. Note the position and reflex point along the diagonal where this happened.

In Celtic lore, the passage from day to night is known as the "crack between the worlds." They believed that the crack was a still point passage or vortex between heaven and earth. The ancient Celtic burial mounds in Ireland contained one window that for years remained a mystery. Then it was discovered that they were built so that the setting sun of the Winter Solstice would align exactly with the window in the burial mound. For a special moment, the sunlight would illuminate the inside of the burial mound and create a still point passageway between the world of the spirits and Earth.

Still points are everywhere because everything comes from and will return to stillness. We have many words, names, and descriptions of our experiences of these moments of stillness. We may spontaneously experience a moment of silence as an inner calmness, or we can experience a deep feeling of inner peace. We can be working, and an unexpected pause in activity brings us a rare moment of quietness. We can be at a party where people are talking, glasses are clinking, and background music is playing when there is an unexpected pause in the conversations. The music stops, and a moment of stillness sweeps through the room.

Be still.

STILL POINT INTERLUDE

The importance of a still point is difficult to comprehend from the mind-set of reaching goals and getting the job done. A moment of stillness, no matter how brief, is a glimpse into forever or what the Taoists referred to

> *"Be Still and Ye Shall Know."*
> — Twenty Third Psalm
>
> *In silence the teachings are heard; In stillness the world is transformed.* — Lao Tzu

as the "Absolute." You can experience this when you meditate on the glass-like surface of a still pond and toss a rock into it, watch as the ripples move outwards and return to the center, creating different patterns. Hold the picture of the still pond in your mind while you simultaneously enjoy the patterns until they return to stillness.

Listen to a wind chime sounding in the breeze. When the breeze enters a still point, the chimes become silent. If you take in the larger picture, the trees or plants may still be moving with the breeze, yet the chimes are silent. They are momentarily in a node of stillness within the breeze. Listen to the silence the way you listened to the sound of the chimes. When the breeze resumes, listen to the chimes as though they were sounding within an ocean of silence.

Himalayan Rishies, or Holy Men, living in caves high in the mountains are awakened every morning by stillness. The night breezes sweep through the mountains, and just as the sun begins to rise, there is an atmospheric shift and the breezes stop. The Himalayan Saints call this moment of stillness between night and day "the Nova Swan." Each morning they are awakened by the silent stillness of the Nova Swan.

The Yaqui Sorcerer, Don Juan, believed he was most powerful at dusk when stillness descended on the Sonoran desert. He called these times of still-ness glimpses into forever. He believed that anything is possible if one departs from inner silence.

Anechoic Reflections

The connection between nervous system tuning and whole body posture can be clearly perceived in the anechoic chamber. The result of my listening to the Perfect Fifth was profound on many levels. At the time, my phenomenological research was based on systematically exploring through my direct experience. I adopted an energy medicine model based on system science protocols to integrate my discoveries into the healing arts. Over the years, I used palpation skills to evaluate hyper- or hypotensions on joints based on an ideal tension related to Perfect Fifth nervous system tuning. I used sound as well as touch therapy and verbal counseling to bring these tensions back into resonance with the ideal sound of the Perfect Fifth. The outcome of the work was profound and I witnessed many healings. I knew there were profound biochemical changes taking place when the nervous system shifted. Because my work involved hands-on therapy with sound, I could feel areas of excess tension relax.

The Biochemical Effect of Tuning Forks on Ideal Nervous System Tuning

Research suggests that vibration transferred to neuronal, endothelial, and immune cells through tuning forks stimulates nitric oxide, and sets off a cascading of physiological events which directly influences our health, well-being, state of mind, and consciousness. By understanding nitric oxide, we can establish a scientific link between molecular science, medicine, and sound healing.

Nitric oxide, which is referred to in an abbreviated version as NO, is a molecule created by a nitrogen atom bound to an oxygen atom. It is one of the smallest molecules found in nature, consisting of one nitrogen atom and one oxygen atom. NO is fundamental to all life—human, animal, insect, and plant. In our human body, nitric oxide is made inside our vascular, nerve, and immune cells. It is then rhythmically released into the surrounding tissues as a gas. NO participates in the healthy function of all main organ systems.

Immune, vascular, and neural cells release a constant level of nitric oxide in rhythmic cycles called "puffing." This basal level of NO relaxes our cells and keeps them in a mildly alert state. When our cells detect viruses, bacteria, or free radicals, they activate and produce more NO. This signals a cascading of biochemical events which destroys viruses, bacteria, and free radicals. For this reason, NO is called a signaling molecule; however, NO by itself also attacks and neutralizes viruses, bacteria, and free radicals. Once the invader is neutralized, NO signals the attack to stop, called "down regulating," which initiates another biochemical cascade, returning our cells to a relaxed alert state.

Researchers term the rhythmic release of nitric oxide by cells "puffing." The release of NO takes place in six minute puffing cycles which are closely linked with the autonomic nervous system. During the three minute rising phase of puffing, NO is released and signals the body to move into parasympathetic mode causing cells to relax, move further apart, thin their walls, and become rounder. During the falling puffing phase, NO dissipates and signals the body to move into sympathetic mode, causing cells to go on alert, cluster together, thicken their cell walls, and become asymmetrical.

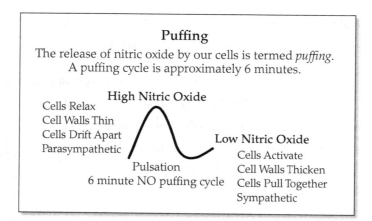

When we are under stress, the sympathetic/parasympathetic balance is often-times thrown off balance. The result is a compromise in NO puffing leading to diminished NO production and in extreme cases, a shutdown in NO production which researchers call "flatlining." Compromised NO production leads to a depressed immune function which over time results in tissue pathology. The process begins as a lack of energy, joint pain, depression, decreased sexual drive, headaches, mild depression, memory loss, and poor digestion. Over a longer period of time, if NO rhythms are not restimulated, these symptoms can escalate into major diseases, including cardiovascular disease, diabetes, Alzheimer's, autoimmune diseases, and cancer.

For example, one of the largest areas of medical research is the role of nitric oxide in cardiovascular disease. Nitric oxide works directly with the endothelial linings of blood vessels. The endothelium is the innermost layer of tissue that lines arteries and blood vessels. The blood vessels in the skin, brain, heart, and all organs are lined with endothelial cells. We have 100,000 miles of blood vessels creating a endothelium surface area larger than a football field.

When endothelium cells are healthy, they puff nitric oxide. In the presence of nitric oxide, blood vessels are pliable, elastic, and able to naturally expand and contract with the pulsation of blood. White blood cells and platelets are able to move freely in the blood stream. Simultaneously, nitric oxide acts as an immune enhancer searching out and destroying opportunistic bacteria, viruses, and free radicals throughout the endothelium.

When an unhealthy endothelium becomes inflamed due to compromised nitric oxide its surface becomes hard and sticky causing white blood cells and platelets to adhere to blood vessel walls leading to atherosclerosis. The consequences of this are far-reaching. For example, research is now being accumulated on Alzheimer's that indicates it is a vascular disorder instead of a neurological one. Capillaries in the brain are compromised due to compromised nitric oxide, resulting in a reduced oxygen and glucose supply to brain cells. Over time this can lead to neurological dysfunction, cellular death, and dementia.

Researchers use the word "spiking" to describe the stimulation and/or reactivation of nitric oxide puffing in cells. Due to stress, nitric oxide puffing can be compromised and needs a stimulus to bring it back into rhythm. Research shows that the a 128 cps tuning fork, which we call an Otto 128,[16] will spike nitric oxide and enhance NO puffing rhythms. This boost of NO balances the autonomic nervous system and signals a natural release of anti-bacterial, anti-virals, and free radicals on a microcellular level.

We experimented with the tuning forks in the lab, trying to measure the effects of sound on human tissues. At first the biochemists could not believe how fast the reaction took place, or that it even took place at all. We repeated the tests many times with many samples, always having the same results. We observed the nitric oxide spiking. The third test was the clincher. I gave a tuning fork to each biochemist and what followed is something I will never forget—three biochemists in white coats tapping their tuning forks and putting them on their bodies to feel the effects. I was elated because I had spent 28 years feeling the effects, and now the reductionist science was finally happening. That day the scientists gave me the nick name "Vibrating John," and a new doorway opened into the understanding of the power of sound to heal.

---

[16] Otto is an abbreviation for osteophonic which means "sound that vibrates bones." See chapter on Osteophonic Tuning Forks.

The following graph shows nitric oxide released by the vibration of a Otto 128.

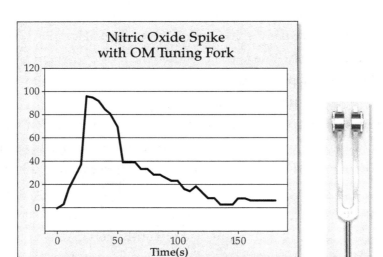

An amperometric system is used to detect and measure NO release. The amperometric system is simply a hollow needle capped with a micro net which only allows NO gas to permeate. The gas is measured via optic connections within the needle that interface with a computer. The system can be used in cellular cultures and can measure the release of NO in real time through monitoring of the blood.

Much can be inferred from an understanding of the Otto 128 tuning fork. The Otto 128 tuning fork is based on the "difference tone" of a Perfect Fifth. It vibrates a Perfect Fifth pulse. For example, the difference between the C256 cps and G384 cps tuning forks is arrived at by subtracting 256 cps from 384 cps which equals 128 cps. This means that when you are listening to a Perfect Fifth, you are hearing a 128 cps pulse that is created between the C and G tuning forks.[17]

Once the vibration of the Otto 128 is introduced into the body, it travels throughout the body as a Perfect Fifth wave. The transmission of sound waves through the body was confirmed in 1990 by Dahl and Grosebek in the *Journal of the Acoustical Society of America*.[18] Investigating the effects of sound on fiber motion, they found that sound waves stimulated any flexible fibrous material,

---

[17] For a better understanding of the Perfect Fifth and its importance read the chapter on Nervous System Tuning.

[18] M. Dahl, E. Rice, and D. Groesbeck. (1990). "Effects of fiber motion on the acoustic behavior of an anisotropic flexible fibrous membrane." *Journal of the Acoustical Society of America*, 87, 416-422.

e.g., nervous and connective tissue throughout the body. Their research supports the claim that tuning fork vibrations can induce resonance in fibrous connective tissues, e.g., muscle, cell membranes, nerves, ganglia, and plexuses (nerve networks) of membranes and nerves, ganglia, and plexuses (nerve networks) of the human body.

When we include "body hearing" through tissue conduction, we are capable of perceiving frequencies far above and far below the normal range of hearing. For example, the tympanic membrane or eardrum stretches across the ear canal within the inner recesses of the temporal bone. This membrane is like a drum head which registers normal sound waves between 16 cps and 20,000 cps as well as vibrations smaller than the wave length of visible light. Lenhardt, Wang, and Clarke reported in *Science* that high frequency acoustic energy can be transmitted along bone tissue and through cell cytoplasm without loss of fidelity.[19]

We believe it is the Perfect Fifth pulse created by the Otto 128 and Perfect Fifth wave created by the C and G tuning forks that tunes the nervous system, spikes nitric oxide, and stimulates the release of antibacterials, antivirals, and free radicals. Ideal nervous system tuning is a perfect balance between the sympathetic and parasympathetic nervous systems. It makes sense that the Perfect Fifth has been known as the interval of perfect balance between yin and yang throughout history. Today we know that nitric oxide regulates and signals perfect balance. The Otto 128 acts through tissue vibration, and the C and G tuning forks act through sound waves to signal the nervous system to come back into balance.

When the nervous system comes into tune and nitric oxide is stimulated, some of the benefits attributed by researchers are: enhanced cell vitality which is the basis of anti-aging, a stabilized body metabolism that regulates digestion and body weight, an enhanced vascular flow leading to increased energy, stamina, sexual drive, enhanced memory, and a greater sense of well being. Furthermore, research has demonstrated that the proper stimulation of NO acts as a preventative to the development of arteriolar sclerosis, stroke, heart attack, diabetes, Alzheimer's, depression, autoimmune disease, and cancer.

---

[19] M. Lenhardt, R. Skellett, P. Wang, and A. Clarke (1991). "Human ultrasonic speech perception." *Science*, 253, 82-85.

PART 2

The Tuning Fork Experience

Anechoic Reflections

I named the original set of Pythagorean tuned tuning forks I used in the anechoic chamber the Solar Harmonic Spectrum. I liked the term "solar" because the tuning forks had a bright sound and rang the full spectrum of overtones. The chamber, due to sensory isolation, could be very disorienting. In order to keep my bearings and know exactly what I was doing, I developed a journal. Every time I went in the chamber, I systematically recorded my experiments with each interval. I spent one week working with each interval. For example, I would listen to the interval of a fifth for one week, and then the next week I would listen to an interval of a fourth and so on.

At one point, I recorded each interval and played them back on speakers on each side of my bed. I would play the interval at a very low volume in order not to disturb my sleep. I kept a dream journal and the next morning I would record my dreams after being in the interval all night. I got so into being in the different intervals that I bought a special headphone called a bonefone. The bonefone goes around your neck and conducts sounds through bone conduction into the ears. This was before iPods and MP3s. I used a Sony Walkman with a cassette to play back the interval on auto reverse.

I would live as much as possible both in and out of the anechoic chamber inside each interval. I called it interval emersion. The more I knew how the sound affected my mind and body, the better I would be able to know how to use it with a patient. The same formula holds true today. The more you experience and know about an interval, the better you will be able to use it with yourself and others. The tuning forks are learning tools that teach you the knowledge of your own nervous system and the effects of different tunings. Once you understand this, the tuning forks become just another way to connect you to the universal field. With practice, you can think the sound of the tuning forks, and your nervous system and body will come into resonance.

Solar Harmonic Spectrum
The Art of Pythagorean Tuning

Pythagoras was a Greek philosopher and mathematician who lived around 580 B.C. He was a contemporary of both Buddha and Confucius and is said to have traveled to Egypt, Mesopotamia, and India in search of knowledge. Pythagoras believed in a "singing universe" which he poetically termed "the music of the spheres." He

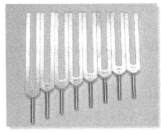

Solar Harmonic Spectrum

taught that musical instruments, especially the lyre, when tuned to Pythagorean intervals were capable of tuning the soul to the singing rhythms of the universe.

The lyre was the main instrument the Pythagoreans used to tune the soul. There are many stories about the Pythagoreans and their use of the lyre. One goes like this.

> *A demented youth forced his way into the dwelling of a prominent judge who had recently sentenced the boy's father to death for a criminal offense. The frenzied lad, bearing a naked sword, approached the jurist, who was dining with friends, and threatened his life. Among the guests was a Pythagorean. Reaching over quietly, he struck an interval upon a lyre which had been laid aside by a musician who had been entertaining the gathering. At the sound of the interval, the crazed young man stopped in his tracks and could not move (still point). He was led away as though in a trance.[1]*

Today, tuning forks are like a modern lyre which is always in tune. Instead of plucking strings to sound Pythagorean intervals, the modern practitioner can tap tuning forks and achieve the same effect without traditional music training. Tuning forks can go beyond the traditional Greek lyre with their ability to create individual sonic spaces and precise overtones.

---

[1] Manley P. Hall, *The Therapeutic Value of Music.* Los Angeles: Philosophical Research Society, 1955, p. 3.

A Pythagorean interval can be visualized as the sonic space defined by two tuning forks. Each Pythagorean interval has unique qualities that effect healing and consciousness. When the listener enters the sonic space created by a Pythagorean interval, he experiences a pulse that entrains the whole body and simultaneously tunes the nervous system. Within seconds the listener experiences a shift in consciousness complete with a new mental, emotional, and physical pattern.

When a Pythagorean interval is sounded, it can be visualized as a gateway of sound inside of which the two tones of the tuning forks merge into a spiral to create a third sound. The third sound is called a difference tone in musical language because it is simply the difference in frequency between the two tuning forks. The Pythagoreans, based on their experience, called the difference tone the "Voice of God." **It is the Voice of God that pulses through the whole body, tunes the nervous system, and energizes the five elements.**

Creating intervals with tuning forks is easy. Musicians spend a lot of time learning scales and combinations of sounds to create music. Interval tuning is much simpler because it focuses on healing rather then musical performance. All that is required is the ability to lay out the tuning forks in order and count from one through eight. Here is how it works.

Set Up

Lay out the Solar Harmonic Spectrum in the order below. When making an interval, always use C256 as the number 1 tuning fork and count up to get the second tuning fork. For example, the space between C256 and G is called the interval of a 5th. If you count the numbers or notes from C256 to G, there will be exactly five notes. When you count up, associate the numbers with the letters, i.e., C and F is the interval of a 4th, C and A is the interval of a 6th and so on.

C256	D	E	F	G	A	B	C512
1	2	3	4	5	6	7	8

Next, select the interval you want to work with. In order to learn how to work with the intervals, begin by selecting the interval of a 5th, C256 and G. In order to sound an interval, you will find there are three components: technique, visualization, and reception. Technique is the method of producing sound. Visualization is what you intend when you produce the sound. Reception is the act of transferring the sound to yourself or someone else for healing.

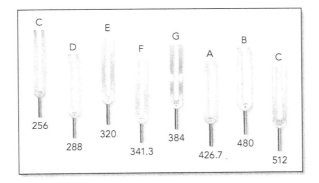

Techniques

KNEE TAP :: Technique 1

1. Hold the tuning forks by the stems with moderate pressure—not too tight and not too loose.
Do not hold your tuning forks by the prongs because the prongs need to vibrate in order to create the sound.

2. Gently tap the flat side of the tuning fork on your kneecap. Do not hit or slap your kneecap with the tuning fork.

All it takes is a gentle yet firm tap and your tuning fork will sound. It is as though you gently drop the flat side of the tuning fork on your kneecap. (If you do not want to tap the forks on your knees, you can tap them on the floor, the side of a massage table, or even the palm of your hand. Some practitioners use a hockey puck strapped to their knee which is awkward but effective.)

It is best to tap the C256 first on one knee and the G tuning fork on the other knee. Once you have mastered the method, you can tap both tuning forks at the same time.

 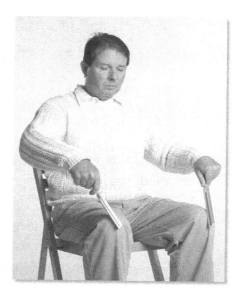

3. Bring the forks slowly to your ears, about three to six inches from your ear canal. Close your eyes and listen.

When the sound stops, lower your tuning forks and switch them from hand to hand. For example, if you listened to the C in your right ear first, than switch it to your left ear for the second tap. Now tap your tuning forks again.

4.   When the sound fades, wait at least fifteen seconds and allow yourself to be with the aftereffects of the tone.

Humming: Anchoring the Sound

Find a safe, quiet place and play the interval you have chosen to work with. While you are inside the interval, hum a sound that resonates within the space of the interval. If you find yourself focusing on the sound of one tuning fork or the other, relax and let your ears find a sound that resonates within the space of both tuning forks. Put down the tuning forks, imagine being in the space of the interval, and hum the sound. Play the interval again and check yourself. Put down the tuning forks and hum the interval sound.

The goal is to develop the ability to hum and shift into the interval anywhere, at will, without having to have the tuning forks.

OVERTONE TAP :: Technique 2

The second way to sound tuning forks is to tap them together. This method is to be used off the body. It is not to be used directly in the ears.

1.   Hold them by the stems and tap them together on their edges, not the flat side of the prongs. You do not have to use a lot of force to get the result. Play with creating an easy sounding tap vs. a banging tap when too much force is used.

2.   When you tap them together, the tuning forks will make sounds we call *overtones*. Move the tuning forks around, slowly and quickly, in the air and listen to the different tones as they get louder and softer. The photos on the following pages demonstrate the movement of the tuning forks over the body. Notice the different positions and their relationship to the body. When you move the tuning forks over the body, it will cause different overtones to ring.

3.   For practice, take the F, G, and A tuning forks and hold them in your left hand.

Place the stems between your fingers. Allow them to stick out in different directions so that they do not touch. Hold the C tuning fork between your thumb and first finger in your right hand. Tap the F, G, and A tuning forks with the C256 tuning fork.

Move the tuning forks around slower and then faster. Then listen to the different over-tones. Try holding the F, G, and A tuning forks on top and the C on the bottom. Move them around, and move the C tuning fork in circles underneath the F, G, and A tuning forks. The movement of the C tuning fork will bring out different overtones.

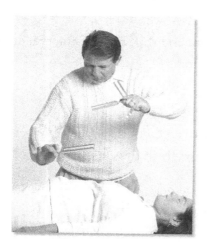
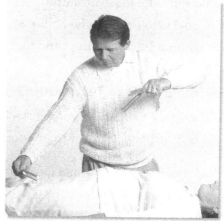

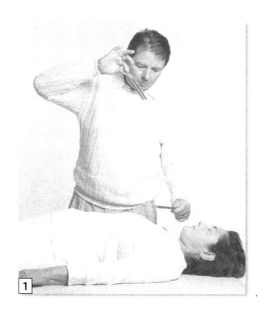

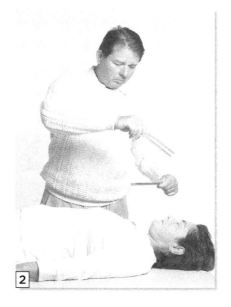

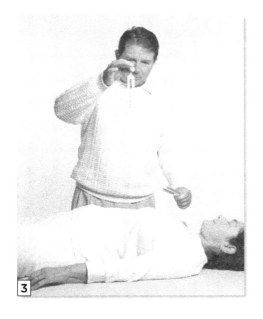

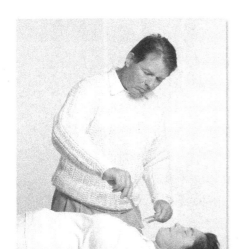

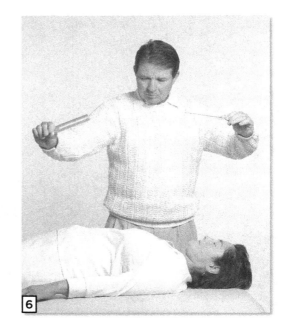

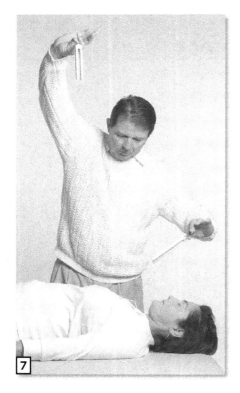

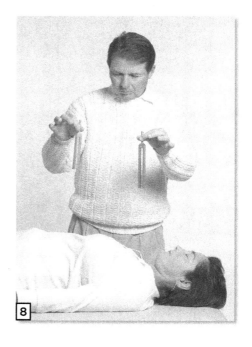

Visualization

Visualization is the act of creating an intention for the sound. The visualization to heal has to be clear before the forks are tapped. Method without visualization is limited. Through visualization, the sound of the tuning forks becomes a deeper healing experience. The following story illustrates this point.

When I was a student at Indiana University, I happened to be in the music auditorium one afternoon. That afternoon a piano concert was to be given by Rudolph Serkin. The piano tuner was tuning, and I was enjoying being the only one in the hall. Since it was dark off stage and I was in the back of the hall, I found it easy to doze off to the tuning sounds. I remember at one point the piano tuner striking middle C over and over. I must have heard him play it thirty or forty times. Then there was a period of silence for two to three minutes. I drifted off in the silence.

Then out of the silence I heard middle C again. This time the note sent shivers up my spine. The sound was completely different, and at the same time I knew the note was the same. Then I heard it again and again. It was like a concert. There was something very special about this middle C. I opened my eyes and to my surprise I saw the piano tuner standing next to the piano. Sitting at the piano playing middle C was Rudolph Serkin, one of the greatest pianists of the 20th century.

1. Before you tap your tuning forks, visualize what you want to accomplish. For example, visualize a positive image and feel the image in your body; ask for the light for the highest good; visualize an element quality; or just picture the feeling of the healing response.

2. Tap the tuning forks and allow the felt feeling of the image to guide your tap and resonate with the sound.

3. Next bring the tuning forks to your ears. Ring them over the body, or place them on the body with the feeling of the visualization as your guide.

Reception: Allowing the sound to shift your vibrational state of being

Reception is the act of relaxing and preparing yourself or someone else to better receive the sound of the tuning forks. A simple way to understand the need for reception is to imagine a tense person trying to listen to a concert. The sounds are coming to them with good technique and visualization; however, they are not being fully received due to inner tension. Over time, the sound may relax the tension and lead to greater receptivity. However, if the person could become relaxed and prepared before the concert, they would be more attuned to the sound.

In the healing arts, there are many ways to create reception. Here are a few ideas.

1. For self-healing, before you work with the tuning forks, sit in a safe place. Next, close your eyes and take a few deep breaths. Allow your thoughts to come and go without focus. If necessary, stretch or tighten a muscle group and then relax. Do this for several minutes and then tap the tuning forks.

2. When working with another, any bodywork method can prepare them for reception. A simple method with the person sitting up is to hold the forehead in one hand and the back of the head (occiput) in the other hand. Take a deep breath and just imagine energy pulsing between your hands. Do this for 2 to 3 minutes, then use the tuning forks.

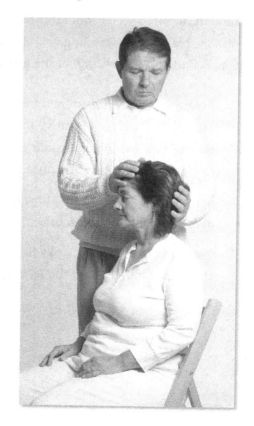

3. With the person laying down, cradle their head in your hands. Make sure they are comfortable and that their head is snug and comfortable in your hands. Do this for two to three minutes. Then use the tuning forks.

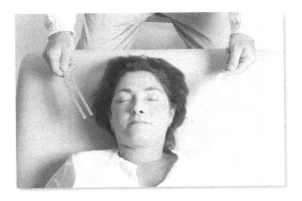

4. After a bodywork session, when a patient is already in a relaxed state, you just need to let them know you are using the tuning forks. This is because the sound may shock them if they are not properly informed. Say something like, "You will be hearing a sound. Just allow your body to relax deeply into the sound and learn what it has to teach you for your healing."

5. If you are using the tuning forks in a psychotherapeutic situation, guided imagery is an excellent reception method. A few words may work. For example, you might say, "Close your eyes and relax. Imagine sitting against an old tree on a mountainside on a clear day. Take a deep breath and listen as some very special birds bring you their sounds."

Solar Harmonic Spectrum Interval Explorations

Interval explorations is an opportunity to learn about and individually experience each interval. The presentation of each interval is divided into sections to help you explore and understand the qualities of each interval. Each interval exploration follows the same organization.

INTERVAL NAME AND RATIO

This is given as a number and/or a name. The ratio is the mathematical relationship between the two tuning forks.

This is a graphic illustration of two tuning forks sounding an interval. This is also called a Lissajous figure. In the mid-19th century, Jules Lissajous, a French mathematician, devised an experiment. He found that if a small mirror was attached at the tip of a tuning fork, and a light beam was aimed at it, the vibration wave pattern of the tuning fork could be thrown onto a dark screen.

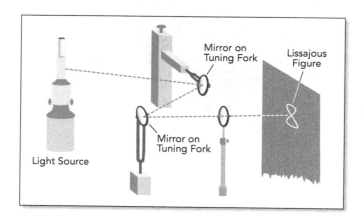

Next, Lissajous projected the light from the mirror of the first tuning fork onto a mirror attached to the tip of a second tuning fork placed at right angles to the first tuning fork. When the two waves were projected onto the dark wall, he discovered that Pythagorean intervals produced beautiful shapes. These shapes are now known as Lissajous figures Today, Lissajous figures are created using an oscilloscope.

Keyboard

The interval is shown on a piano keyboard. Although the intervals are Pythagorean and not tuned to a normal keyboard tuning, the keyboard is presented as a general reference to get the feeling of space between the tones.

ELEMENT ACTIVATED BY INTERVAL

This section gives the element interval relationships. The intervals created by the Pythagorean tuning forks are like the two intertwining snakes of the caduceus. The crisscrossing pattern of an interval is clearly seen in the Lissajous figures.

Just as the intertwining snakes of the caduceus create positive and negative polarities generated from a neutral core, the tones of the tuning forks pulsate in positive, negative, and neutral polarities. The positive and negative polarities of an interval can be described in many ways including expanding (+) and contracting (–), rising (+) and falling (–), ascending (+) and descending (–). They are generated from a neutral center called the Comma of Pythagoras. The Comma of Pythagoras is eliminated in modern tuning systems.

For example, the Air element is activated by the intervals of a fifth (+) and a fourth (–). A way of visualizing the + and – qualities is to breathe in and out. Inhalation corresponds to moving energy earthwards to the (–) pole. When a newborn comes into the world, its first breath is an inhalation which pulls its consciousness into its body. The exhalation of air (+) moves our consciousness upwards and gives us more space or Ether (+). When we pass away, the last thing we do is exhale air and return to the Universal Energy Field.

The relationship between Ether Element and Earth Element is that Ether is (+) and Earth is (–). Energy moves from the Universal Energy Field to the negative pole which is Mother Earth. It ascends upwards through the positive (+) pole, Ether, to a neutral center. For this reason, Earth corresponds to unison, or one tone. In the Solar Harmonic Spectrum set of Pythagorean tuning forks Earth this is represented by the base C tone of 256 cps. The base C tone can also be lowered one octave to the Otto 128 tone. Earth can also be hummed as a low drone tone in resonance with the Otto 128.

This can be seen clearly in the Pythagorean scale. The Ether and Earth Elements, which represent the space between heaven and earth, set the positive, neutral, and negative polarity of the whole scale.

Ether (+) ---------------------------------- Earth (–)

The elements of Air, Fire, and Water then pulsate between Ether and Earth in positive and negative polarities. This is why Air, Fire, and Water have two intervals that resonate the same element. For example, the positive (+) polarity of Air is the interval of a 5th and the negative (–) Polarity of Air is the interval of a 4th. Both intervals resonate with Air; however, the negative Polarity is associated with Earth and the positive polarity is more associated with Ether. What is important is not whether an element is positive or negative, but rather the balance of that element with its neutral center.

The Fire element is activated by the intervals of a 6th and 3rd. The 6th is ascending Fire. Edgar Cayce, the sleeping prophet, referred to the 6th as the interval of mystics ascending or rising to higher states of consciousness. The interval of a 3rd is a more earthly Fire which has to do with daily drive and motivation. The Water element is activated by the intervals of a 7th and 2nd. The 7th is an interval of higher creative processes and was called "Dew from Heaven" by the alchemists. The 2nd is an interval that inspires creative thinking for our everyday challenges.

Sounding and Journaling

The Sound Journal is located in Appendix A. The purpose of keeping a Sound Journal is to organize your experiences so that you can better know the qualities of each interval. The more you understand about an interval, the better you will know how to use it for healing. It is suggested that you find a safe place and work with the interval using the knee tap, humming, and overtone methods. The humming anchors-in the experience of the interval and allows you to tune into the interval at any time without tuning forks. We suggest you photocopy the journal and create a new journal page for each interval session. The journal questions provided are suggestions. Feel free to discover and create new inquiries.

The Intervals

THE INTERVAL OF AN OCTAVE:
The Space between Heaven and Earth

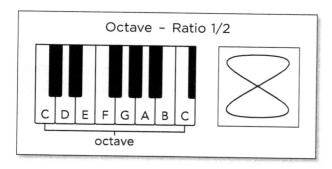

ELEMENT: Ether

COLOR: blue

BENEFITS: Space, openness, joint flexibility, freedom of expression; balances sacrum with occiput.

Octave comes from "octa" which means eight. The octave starts with C and ends with the same note, C, eight notes higher. The octave contains the 8 notes: C, D, E, F, G, A, B, C, which make up the Western musical scale. However, the space of the octave is much larger than eight notes and contains an infinite number of possibilities and divisions. The Greeks called the octave *diapason* which means "through all."

The octave represents the beginning and ending of a complete cycle. The cycle of an octave is important to modern science as well as the psychology of consciousness. When the Buddha obtained illumination under the Bodhi tree, he announced the Noble Eightfold Path of enlightenment. Patanjali, the great Indian sage, created the eight "limbs" of yoga necessary for union with the divine. In these spiritual systems, one begins with Earth, which is analogous to the lower tone of the octave and progresses through the eight stages to enlightenment represented by the higher note of the octave.

> The lower and higher tones of the Octave represent the polarization of opposites—the alpha and omega, moon and sun, male and female, yin and yang, mother and father. The *Emerald Tablet of Hermes*, one of the oldest Alchemical texts, can be summarized by the statement, "as Above, so Below."

In other words, the beginning of the octave, the C below, resonates with the ending of octave, the C above. This principle of opposites is repeated in all major religions. For example, in Christianity the Lord's Prayer says "Thy will be done on Earth (below) as in Heaven (above)."

Scientists have used the principle of the octave in many ways. Johannes Kepler, the German astronomer and mathematician, discovered the laws of planetary motion through an understanding of the octave. In the 1860s, English chemist John Newland, showed that all the chemical elements fall into eight families. His Periodic Table of the Elements hangs in every highschool chemistry class today. Nikolai Tesla, the inventor and physicist, discovered the alternating current generator which unleashed the modern technological revolution after a series of visions in which he "saw" that everything in the universe obeys the law of octaves.

Today, marine biologists studying dolphins use the octave to bring their high-pitched sounds into the range of human hearing. They record dolphins singing and slow down the recordings so that the listener hears the sounds one to two octaves lower than the dolphins. Astronomers use radio telescopes to listen to the sounds of space and raise or lower sounds by octaves in order to bring them into the range of human hearing. One can actually hear the music of the spheres using the principle of the octave.

THE INTERVAL OF A PERFECT FIFTH:
Air Rising to Heaven

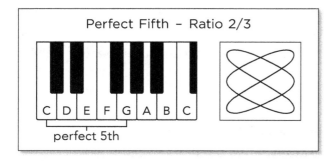

ELEMENT: Air (+)

COLOR: blue green

BENEFITS: Lifts depression; joint mobility; balances earth with spirit; general tonic; directly stimulates nitric oxide release; antibacterial, antiviral, and immune enhancement; balances heart; balances pituitary gland and releases opiate and canniboid receptor sites in the third ventricle of the brain; balances sphenoid bone; balances sympathetic and parasympathetic nervous system.

(See the chapter Ideal Nervous System Tuning: The Perfect Fifth for an explanation of the Perfect Fifth)

THE INTERVAL OF A FOURTH:
Air Descending to Earth

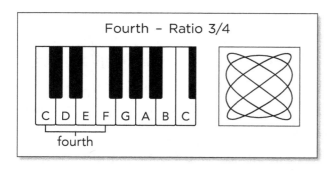

ELEMENT: Air (–)

COLOR: green

BENEFITS: Brings us back to reality; stabilizes hyper, obsessive, and or manic thought processes; balances lower bowel; balances the fourth ventricle of the brain and releases opiate receptors in fourth ventricle; down-regulates amygdala; balances temporal bones and TMJ release. The interval of a fourth is a grounding interval for our thoughts.

Leonardo DaVinci's famous drawing, Squaring the Circle, graphically shows the relationship between the octave, fourth and fifth. The circle represents the octave or heaven. The square with four sides represents Earth. The man in between balances heaven and earth when he is in the five star pattern which is the interval of a fifth.

It is interesting to note that the playing of octaves, fourths, and fifths are common to all cultures. Gregorian chants are primarily the octaves, fourths, and fifths. Primitive drummers always beat one, four, five rhythms. Popular music and Country Western music is based on the same progressions.

THE INTERVAL OF A SIXTH:
Ascension, Fire Rising to Heaven

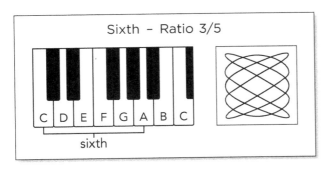

ELEMENT: Fire Ascending

COLOR: yellow orange

RATIO: 3/5

BENEFITS: Spiritual visions; works with moods by clearing our past processes including past lives and lifts our spirit; gives insight into problem solving by "getting out of the box"; stimulates pineal gland and release of visionary molecules; works with migraine headaches located around eyes; aids in memory retention.

The interval of a sixth is the interval of mystical Fire and ascension of Spirit. The sixth can be symbolized as the Phoenix rising from the ashes. The alchemists called the interval of the sixth "the Sacred Fire." Listening to the sixth was said to burn away any impurities of mind and body into a Sacred Ash (Earth), allowing our spirits to rise into the higher realms. In Christianity, the sixth represents the ascension of Christ to Heaven. Edgar Cayce called the sixth the interval of mysticism. The sixth is the interval of vision and inspiration which opens gateways into our dreams.

THE INTERVAL OF A THIRD:
Alchemic Furnace, Fire Descending to Earth

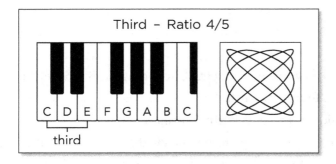

Third – Ratio 4/5

ELEMENT: Fire Descending
COLOR: yellow
RATIO: 4/5

BENEFITS: Motivation; focus on goal; getting things done; balances liver and upper GI tract; stimulates digestion, improves sexual drive; balances respiratory diaphragm.

The interval of a third is the Fire of life. The third builds an internal fire that motivates and moves us towards our goals. The interval of a third warms us and resonates with our fire of accomplishment. When we are down and we need to focus on something that we want, the interval of a third will wake us up. The fire illuminates our goal and burns the inner fuel that drives us to take action.

The alchemists called the interval of a third the Alchemic Fire because it heats us and separates the five elements. It is like the fire the alchemists built beneath their alchemic furnaces for their experiments. Listening to the third heats our internal alchemic furnace causing the five elements to activate, separate, and slowly transform into our goals.

THE INTERVAL OF A SEVENTH:
Sacred Dew, Water Rising to Heaven

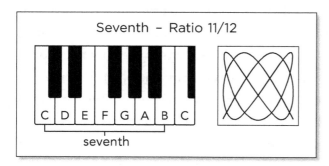

Seventh – Ratio 11/12

ELEMENT: Water Ascending
COLOR: red orange
RATIO: 11/12

BENEFITS: Balances the parietal bones; releases cranial sutures; stimulates cerebro-spinal fluid flow; shapes inspirations into dream forms.

The seventh is like warm steam rising. The seventh carries the essence of our vision up into the higher realms. It is the interval of sacred moisture which vibrates with our inspiration. The seventh is the last ascending interval and seeks to complete our journey by merging with the higher tone or octave.

The alchemists said that the interval of a seventh represented the Sacred Moisture that massaged and entered the Philosopher's Stone. The seventh is our higher inspirations in pure form. Edgar Cayce called the seventh the "interval of ideals." Imagine a slide projector shining light through a slide. The slide is our ideal pattern which is projected onto the screen. The screen represents our earthly self and the light represents the higher octave.

In our cranium, the seventh relates to our lateral ventricles, parietal bones, and the movement of cerebrospinal (water) fluid through our cranial sutures and dura. The seventh resonates the frontal, central parietal, temporal, and occiput sutures allowing our parietal bones to lift and open like the petals of a flower to the higher light. When this happens, our inner steam is released from our mortal coil and rises upwards, through the seventh chakra, in spiral motions.

THE INTERVAL OF A SECOND:
Dew from Heaven Water Falling to Earth

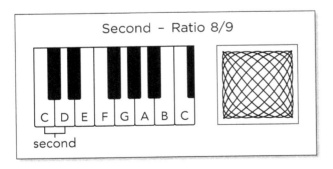

Second – Ratio 8/9

second

ELEMENT: Water Descending

COLOR: orange

RATIO: 8/9

BENEFITS: Balances genital-urinary system; stimulates lymphatics to discharge; enhances creative thinking and interrupts cyclic thinking processes; balances ovaries; promotes fertilization and enhances attachment of fetus to uterine wall; enhances sexual excitement and relationship bonding.

The second is the interval of creativity and bonding. As Fire dissolves bonds, the second creates bonds. Ideally, the second creates a higher ideal. It is represented by a mother bonding to her child or an artist working to manifest his vision. The

Alchemists called the second "dew from heaven" because it was like water embedded in an ideal pattern.

Listening to the second may sound dissonant. This is just a matter of taste. Take some time, relax, and get into the space created by the interval of a second.

UNISON:
Mother Earth

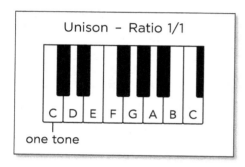

ELEMENT: Earth

COLOR: red

RATIO: 1/1

BENEFITS: Settles emotions; stimulates ganglion of impar to promote sympathetic/parasympathetic nervous system balance; centering; disperses scattered thoughts; balances illeosecal valve and lower bowel; relaxes perineal floor; good for cramps, period, muscle, spastic colon, and colitis.

Unison is not an interval. It is one tone played in both ears. You can create unison by using several methods. The first method is to hum a low-pitched sound. The second is to tap C256 and hold next to one ear and then the other. The third way and best way is to use two Otto 128 tuning forks. (Refer to Otto Tuning Fork chapter.)

Unison is the lower note of the octave without the upper note. Unison is the ground. When a farmer holds earth in his hands, feels its warmth and smells its deep aroma, he becomes one with earth. This is unison. We become one. We are united.

Unison as Earth is a low tone or a drone. Listening to long low tones bring us into our body. We feel grounded. Ideally, unison should be a low-pitched ongoing drone sound.

ELEMENT JOURNEY INTERLUDE

BEFORE THE BEGINNING   *Imagine that before you exist, there is a potential to be you that is floating in a pulsating, undulating, ocean of universal energy. Your potential is unbounded, free, and can expand effortlessly in all directions and in all dimensions. One day, like a chick hatching from an egg, you become like a butterfly emerging from a cocoon, or like Parsifal leaving the dark forest. You realize it is time to take a cosmic journey. Instantly your potential contracts and you are being conceived as a human being. The journey begins. We are forever evolving and looking to bring ourselves into alignment with the great ocean of Sound or Universal Energy Field.*

ETHER   *As you expand from the first contraction, you enter the space of Ether. Your free spirit begins to etherealize in space as a form. You were potential before, and now you are something. For the first time, you begin to experience the beginnings of boundaries. You have no idea what a boundary is, yet you know that your space is defined. You experience your first emotion—Grief. You have lost the pureness of your potential and your grief is so intense that it is impossible to sustain. You want to go back, and there is no going back.*

AIR   *Ether involuntary contracts and then expands. You are breathing the cosmos and discovering the element of Air. For the first time, you feel the emotion of desire. You desire your spirit back and wish for everything to be as it was before. The search begins for your spirit and you look everywhere and as fast as you can. The desire intensifies and you continue to look and look in every direction.*

FIRE   *You expand and there is relief for a moment. As you contract again, your search is so frantic that your movement rubs the ethereal substance, creating a friction, and you enter the element of Fire. The heat builds and builds with the powerful and consuming frustration of not finding your potential. You* are burning, and for the first time you feel the emotion of anger. The Fire and anger intensifies until it becomes a primal scream: "I want my spirit back!"

WATER   The energy expands and there is a sense of relief as it seems you have returned to your potential. Then, without warning, it contracts again, and you enter the element of Water. The intense heat of your Fire has melted the ethereal substance contained within the Air and transformed it into Water. Everything begins to cool down, and the element of Water begins to take on a shape of an image of your lost spirit. Instantly you feel the emotion of attachment. You are in love with the image you have created and, like Narcissus looking at his image reflected in water, you are in a trance.

EARTH   You relax and expand and involuntarily the energy contracts again. You cannot let go of your image and lose your spirit again. Automatically, you feel the emotion of fear and you constrict in order to hold on to your image. Your fear pulls your image together and gives it a solid shape. Your image is real and you are experiencing the Earth element.

Creating Five Element Tuning Fork Sessions with Pythagorean Tuning Forks

Creating a tuning fork element session requires evaluating the elements and then choosing an element combination that is right for yourself or the person with whom you are working. There is no set formula for evaluating the elements. The movement of the elements is a mobile, ever-changing interaction of the elements between the self, the external environment, and the Universal Energy Field. There is only an individual's ability to participate with each element at any given moment.

Illness takes place when element flexibility is lost. When an element transition does not take place, the elements seeking natural expression are held or suppressed. This process begins in the mind. The mind is the conductor of the elements. When the mind is neutral, it is capable of allowing every element to move through as necessary. If the mind takes on a charge, then it's neutrality is lost, resulting in the suppression of an element or elements.

The elements are not good or bad. Nature has no morals or ethics. The mind creates morals and ethics that may or may not be in alignment with the movement of the elements. These morals can become belief systems that lead to judgments and restriction of behavior. For example, an individual will not raise his voice because he judges loudness as "bad." He reasons that his father is loud, and he is not going to be like his father. On an elemental level, he judges the Fire element as bad; and therefore, consciously and unconsciously holds back any Fiery expression. Externally, he remains polite and quiet. He will not get loud under any circumstances. When the elements are suppressed, they will seek other forms of expression that may be unproductive to the individual. In the above instance, the Fire eventually sought somatic expression in the form of an ulcer. The ulcer irritated the man so much he said he just "wanted to scream."

The tuning forks resonate with the elements and create an elemental pattern. When the pattern is focused, based on an evaluation of the elements, correct visualization, and good technique, an element resonance will result that empowers the mind to better conduct the elements. There are many different methods to evaluate the five elements. All are valid and can be used to create element sessions. Ultimately, all of them work together as one method. For learning purposes, the method of evaluation is presented for each element.

METHOD I: Five Element Sessions Using Solar Harmonic Spectrum Tuning Forks

The first method of creating a five element tuning fork session is to use protocols. A protocol session combines the five elements in combinations that supports the desired outcome. Protocol sessions are easy to perform and are excellent methods for learning to create individual element sessions. When you perform a protocol session, visualize and focus on the felt feeling of the desired outcome before tapping the tuning forks. Just tapping the tuning forks will have an effect; however, visualization is important in order to create a healing response.

The protocols can be performed using the knee tap or overtone tap techniques (refer to Solar Harmonic Spectrum chapter). When using the knee tap technique, crisscross the tuning forks by switching them from one ear to the other and back again. For example, if C is held by the left ear and G by the right ear, then on the next tap hold C in the right ear and F in the left ear. The crossing pattern continues throughout the protocol. If you want to extend a protocol then cross each interval. Cross C in the left ear and G in the right ear then C in the right ear and G in the left ear before going to the next interval.

When using the overtone technique, the forks can be tapped in any sequence, allowing them to sound in concert with each other. You can use the 256 fork to direct the energy of the sound field and move the forks around in different directions. You can determine the directions of the movement of your tuning forks to bring out different overtones. In general, let your ears be your guide with this method.

NERVOUS SYSTEM BALANCE AND WELL-BEING :: Protocol #1
- 5th C–G
- 4th C–F
- 6th C–A
- 5th C–G

This is my favorite protocol because it is very similar to the Gregorian chants. When in doubt, always use this protocol. The 5th balances the Air element for clarity of mind and nervous system attunement. The 4th further balances the Air element and calms immediate materialistic thoughts and needs. The 6th gives spiritual insight and renews energy for reaching dreams. The 5th brings every-thing back into balance and focus.

MOTIVATION :: Protocol #2

- 5th C–G
- 3rd C–E
- 6th C–A
- 5th C–G
- 3rd C–E

The 5th balances Air and the nervous system. The Air fuels the 3rd which activates descending Fire for goal motivation. The 6th activates ascending Fire for excitement and breakthrough. The 5th rebalances the air element and fuels the 3rd to keep the momentum going.

INCREASING CREATIVITY :: Protocol #3

- 5th C–G
- 7th C–B
- 2nd C–D
- 6th C–A
- 5th C–G

The 5th activates Air which balances the mind and nervous system. The 7th activates ascending Water leading to the creative source. The 2nd activates descending Water to ground the ascending Water and bring the creative impulse into daily reality. The 6th activates ascending Air for heating the Water with creative vision. The 5th rebalances the nervous system and brings ideas and focus to the creative impulse.

LIFE DIRECTION :: Protocol #4

- Unison Otto 128 & Otto 128 and/or hum a low drone tone
- Octave   C–C512
- 6th   C–A
- 6th   C–A
- 5th   C–G
- 3rd   C–E

The Unison of the Otto 128s and/or humming a low drone tone creates a strong earth grounding. The Octave opens space, and the 6th is repeated two times for vision and insight. The 5th brings vision and insight back into balance, and the 3rd promotes action.

CALMING ANXIETY :: Protocol #5

- Octave   C – C512
- 4th   C – F
- 5th   C – G
- 4th   C – F
- Unison   Otto 128 & Otto 128 and/or hum a low drone tone

The octave creates an Ether space allowing thoughts to become more detached. The 4th balances daily thoughts. The 5th changes the thought pattern to a new pattern more in alignment with the universal energy field. The unison Earth tone brings a sense of security and safety.

DREAMING :: Protocol #6

- 3rd C – E
- 5th C – G
- 6th C – A
- 5th C – G

The 3rd balances the Fire of the day and burns up any excess Air. The 5th Balances the Air for sleep. The 6th suggests positive dreaming which is reinforced by Air quality of the 5th.

QUALITY SLEEP :: Protocol #7

- 3rd C – E
- 4th C – F
- 2nd C – D
- 5th C – G

The 3rd balances the Fire of the day and burns up any excess Air. The 4th balances the Air of daily thoughts. The 2nd brings the attention to the body for physical healing, and the 5th balances Air bringing new thought patterns to reinforce the healing process.

DIGESTIVE BALANCE :: Protocol #8

- 3rd   C – E
- 4th   C – F
- Octave C – C512
- 5th   C – G

The 3rd, Fire, paces the excess Fire from the stress of the day. The 4th – Air, balances the air element in the digestive track. The Octave gives more space for peristaltic movement. The 5th rebalances the nervous system for optimal digestion. The protocol should be performed above the digestive track when using overtone technique. In addition, the Otto 128 can be used on the ASIS (top of the hip bone or anterior superior illiac spine) or along the digestive track. (See the chapter on osteophonic tuning forks.)

LOSS/GRIEF WITH TENDENCY TO THINK :: Protocol #9

- Octave C – C512
- 6th   C – A
- 4th   C – F
- 5th   C – G

The octave opens up the space of Ether and the 6th paces the Fire that keeps the thoughts going in the spiritual realms. The 4th balances those thoughts and helps bring them towards Earth and understanding. The 5th brings an overall sense of balance between loss and earth allowing energy to move freely back and forth as necessary.

LOSS/GRIEF WITH TENDENCY TOWARDS ANGER :: Protocol #10

- Octave C – C512
- 3rd   C – E
- 7th   C – B
- 4th   C – F

The octave opens up the space of Ether and the 3rd paces the Fire/Anger. The 7th brings Water and a soothing insight into the anger. The 4th reorganizes thoughts and allows a new perspective for understanding the anger.

GROUNDING :: Protocol #11
- Unison   C128 – C128 (or hum low drone tone)
- 4th   C – F
- Unison   C128 – C128

METHOD II: Intuition

The second method of creating an element tuning fork session is using your intuition. In the intuitive method, we tune into the energy and ask what elements need attention. The word intuition implies the ability to understand something immediately without the need for conscious reasoning. It comes from Middle English and represents spiritual insight or immediate spiritual communication. The structure for using intuition is as follows.

1. Make sure you are in a safe environment.

2. Relax and open your mind. During sessions, intuitive information can come into your consciousness at any time. This can only happen when the practitioner is relaxed and open to the information.

3. Ask for the light for the highest good. This serves as a filter that only allows information that is safe to come through the intuitive communications. You must trust that whatever comes through is what is right for healing at that time.

4. Tune into the elements and ask what is most important for your intuition to perceive. Be open to the answer. Intuition works quickly; you may get "Fire and Water" and not understand why. Do not question or judge. Just go with what you get. For example, you may get a picture of Fire, a feeling of warmth, a vision of Fire warming Water, or a simple command from an inner voice saying "go with Fire and Water." In this case, create an element session emphasizing Fire and Water.

5. To choose between the + or – element qualities, just ask. For example, you may get Fire and then ask whether it is + or –. If you get a strong "yes" or feeling of "yes," go with it.

METHOD III: Tuning In

The third method of creating an element tuning fork session is called Tuning In. This method relies on your ability to tune into and sense energy movement by sensing the "feeling tone" quality of an element. For example, Earth is a slow feeling contrasted to the fast jumpy feeling of Air. By tuning into an element, it is possible to arrive at an element evaluation that can be used to create a tuning fork session.

1. Hold your hand above each chakra and tune into the element energy.

2. Rate the energy from 1 to 10 with 1 being the least intense and 10 being the most intense. Do this for each element and either graph and/or visualize the peaks and valleys. Feel free to go back and reevaluate a chakra whenever you feel it is necessary.

3. Simultaneously sense the element energy quality of the element. For example, is the Fire a raging fire, glowing ember fire, a spark, very low or even difficult to detect? Do this for each element and during the process determine the + or − quality, i.e., whether you will use a 3rd or 6th to work with the Fire element.

4. Create an element story that is congruent with your element assessment. You may visualize a glowing fire radiating warmth (3rd Fire −) in a large room (Octave Ether). Or, you may visualize a waterfall flowing freely allowing the mind to travel with the sound (+ Water 7th) on a warm Sunny day (+ Fire 6th).

5. Create a strategy for an element session based on the above information. The two primary strategies are:

    Strategy 1: Work with the weakest element(s). For example, if the weakest element is Water, give a tuning fork session which emphasizes the Water element.

    Strategy 2: Work with the strongest element and then move into the weakest element. For example, if Fire is strong and Air is weak then start with Fire Element and lead into the Air Element during the session. This strategy is called pacing and leading.

METHOD IV: Asking

The fourth method of creating an element tuning fork session is to ask what element or elements you, or the person with whom you are working, need right now. It is like shopping for yourself or someone else. You know you need something, and you look over the products until you find one that matches your need. In this case, tune into the energy and ask, "What elements do I need?" For example, if you are excited about reaching a goal, this could be supported by the Fire element. If you haven't clearly defined the goal, then you may want to work with Earth and + Fire. If the goal is defined, then – Fire (a 3rd) would work well. Or, you may choose to mix the Fire with Water to create a creative steam out of which creative goals and the power of motivation can arise. Make sure the element or elements you pick are a match. When you shop for something, you know it is "right" because something "clicks" and there is an inner knowing. The same process will happen when you tune into the elements and visualize the right element combination for your life. When the element and its quality are just right, there will be an inner knowing.

METHOD V: Element Story Analysis

Element story analysis is the logical deduction of elemental patterns based on the knowledge of the behavioral qualities for each element. A story, story fragment, dream, or fantasy can be elementally analyzed based on its theme and word content. Here are some examples.

- STORY: My friend left me.
  GENERAL THEME: Loss
  PRIMARY ELEMENT: Ether
  WORD/PHRASE THEME: My friend; bonding, closeness; Water Element
  ELEMENTS NOT STRONGLY PRESENT: Air, Fire, and Earth

- STORY: I like to go as fast as I can on the exercise machine.
  GENERAL THEME: Motivation/Pushing Oneself
  PRIMARY ELEMENT: Fire with Air
  WORD/PHRASE THEME: N/A
  ELEMENTS NOT STRONGLY PRESENT: Ether, Water, and Earth

- STORY: At first I wanted to go to the movies, then I wanted to stay home, and then I thought maybe we could go bowling or maybe we should just get something to eat.

  THEME: Lots of things to do at the same time

  PRIMARY ELEMENT: Air with Fire

  WORD/PHRASE THEME: I and we; friendship and action. At first I wanted and in the end we wanted; Water in the Air.

  ELEMENTS NOT PRESENT: Ether, Earth

- STORY: I want to play the piano.

  THEME: Doing something important for oneself

  PRIMARY ELEMENT: Air with Fire

  The Air element is primary because of the word "want." A want is a desire that does not exist yet.

  WORD/PHRASE THEME: "I want to play the piano" is a future action and implies an inward visualization of oneself in the future playing the piano. Visualization requires Fire, the imagination of the motivation to learn the piano.

  ELEMENTS NOT PRESENT: Ether, Earth, Water

  ELEMENT DISCUSSION: What elements will we arrive at when we can play the piano? The playing of the piano implies a skill (Earth) which empowers our creative expression (Water). Or, perhaps playing the piano is a theme for "being seen and heard." (Fire – getting out there)

When creating a session for another person, the process depends on your knowledge of their needs and your ability to translate that knowledge into elements. There are levels of needs, and layer upon layer of elemental combinations to meet those needs. Again, it is like shopping. The store is filled with products to meet thousands and thousands of needs at different times. A product may work and lead to yet another level of need. For example, you find the right lawn mower only to realize you need a weed whacker to really do the job right. The same is true with the elements. You create a combination based on what you are receiving, and this may lead to another combination.

Anechoic Reflections

I lost my sense of normal reality when I sat in the anechoic chamber for long periods of time. The sounds of the tuning forks transported me to alternate realities. At the time, I thought of it like a radio station where the tuning fork sounds were like a carrier wave in which embedded within it are multiple realities. When I went inside an interval, I experienced realities within realities. I met many teachers and wise beings who taught me things about myself, sound, and the very nature of reality.

Outside the anechoic chamber, my connection to alternate realities continued. It was as though the anechoic chamber was the teaching environment. Once the lessons were learned, it was possible to transition to an alternate reality at any time. I often continued my alternate reality experiences when dreaming, daydreaming, or becoming aware of something in normal reality that suddenly transported me to an alternate reality. It was not uncommon to be aware of several realities simultaneously. This story happened in the summer of 1974 during the height of my anechoic chamber experiments.

I was walking down a New York street with two friends. The trucks were idling, and the workers were unloading crates. Something about the sound of the trucks caught my attention. I asked my friends if they would be willing to watch out for my safety while I sat down and listened more deeply to the sound of the trucks.

I sat in a safe spot and allowed my body and mind to relax. The sound of the trucks formed a distinct rhythm: da-da-da---boom, da-da-da---boom, etc. I let myself go with the sound. At first I imagined being a teenager in Indiana, and going to the drag races, and listening to the engines idle. I remembered how these sounds fascinated me, and I imagined driving a race car.

Listening, even more deeply to the sound, I felt myself "move inside" its pulse. My imagination and memories were still present now accompanied by a new sensation. A profound quietness or stillness came and, for a moment, I experienced myself just being the sound.

Then there was a shift in my awareness, and I found myself with a group of Australian Aborigine chanters. They were communicating a message about "dream time." I was just as clearly with them as I had been with the truck just a few minutes ago. I allowed myself to absorb their message. An old man signaled that they must move on into the desert. I understood.

At that moment my friend tapped me on my shoulder. I came back to the reality of the New York City street, as the truck drove away.

Sound, Consciousness, and Fibonacci Tuning Forks

The Fibonacci Tuning Forks are designed to resonate with the pathway of consciousness from the sphenoid/pituitary axis to the pineal gland. Their main purpose is to open gateways into alternate realities and to explore higher states of consciousness in order to empower a creative healing response. For this reason, they are excellent sound healing instruments, especially when they are used for working with creativity, vision quests, addictions, and healing traumas.

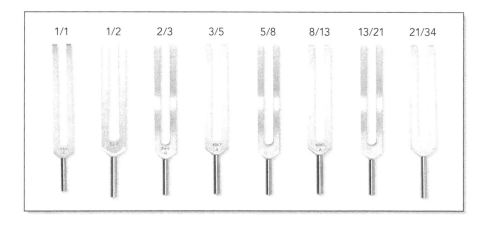

| 1/1 | 1/2 | 2/3 | 3/5 | 5/8 | 8/13 | 13/21 | 21/34 |

Intuitively, the Fibonacci Series tuning forks are precisely tuned seashells. They are based on the spirals found in seashells. When we put a seashell to our ears and listen to the sound, we are like Dorothy riding the vortex of the cyclone to the alternate reality of Oz. Inside the seashell we discover realities within realities. We can spend hours walking the beach collecting shells and listening to their sounds.

The seashell spiral can be translated into a number sequence called the Fibonacci Series which can in turn be translated into a set of tuning forks. The Fibonacci Series starts with zero and one and grows by adding to itself. The last two terms in the sequence are added together to produce the next term. Here is how it works. 0 + 1 = 1, 1 + 1 = 2, 2 + 1 = 3, and so on as follows:

$$0, 1, 1, 2, 3, 5, 8, 13, 21, 34, 55, 89, 144 \ldots$$

The numbers of the Fibonacci Series can be translated into tuning fork sounds by their interval relationships. A Fibonacci interval is any Fibonacci number divided by one adjacent to it in the series. For example, 2/3 is a Fibonacci ratio, as is 3/5, 5/8 and 8/13 and so on.

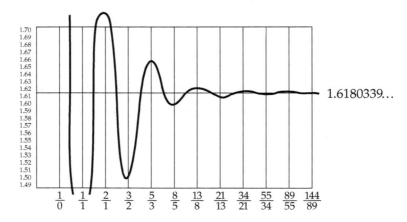

The intervals begin with large pulsations rising far above, then under the center line. They get closer and closer to the center line as the interval pulsations get finer. The interval pulsation will never merge with the center line because the center line is beyond interval and pulse. It is the center of a spiral.

The following chart shows the intervals and their number equivalents.

$$1/1 = 1$$
$$1/2 = 0.5000$$
$$2/3 = 0.66666$$
$$3/5 = 0.60000$$
$$5/8 = 0.62500$$
$$8/13 = 0.615384$$
$$13/21 = 0.619047$$
$$21/34 = 0.617647$$
$$34/55 = 0.618055$$

The further along we go into the sequence, the more the numbers come into alignment with a mathematical/spiritual proportion known as the Golden Mean. Mathematicians define the Golden Mean with numbers; however, it is more an intuitive sense of "right proportion" or "harmony." The number value given to the Golden Mean is .6180339887...n. The dots and the letter "n" mean that the Golden Mean numbers go on forever without any logical sequence. Mathematicians call this an irrational number. We perceive these numbers as a spiral.

The Golden Mean has been called by many names including the Golden Ratio, the Golden Section, the Perfect Division, the Divine Proportion and simply the Greek letter Phi Φ. We intuitively enter the spiral of the Golden Mean through the harmony of the Perfect Fifth. We visually experience it in the spirals of seashells, the patterns of flowers, and in the spiraling galactic systems.

The center of the spiral created by the Golden Mean is a still point. A still point is a place of "no-thingness" or energy without form. Today scientists might refer to it as the "Zero Point."

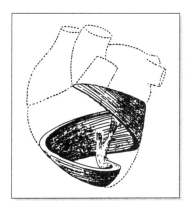

The Golden Mean spiral can be seen throughout the human body. The embryo, the heart, and the ear are of particular interest. The embryo grows along spiral lines of force as it literally spins into life. The heart, when properly dissected, unfolds into a spiral.

The outer ear and the inner ear, called the cochlea, create a spiral within a spiral. The outer ear resembles an embryo and is used by ear acupuncturists as a map for the whole body. A body within a body is the same as a spiral within a spiral going on forever. Body therapists call the art of working with the whole body through a part of the body reflexology. In many instances, working with the colon points of the ears to heal a colon spasm may be more effective than working directly on the colon.

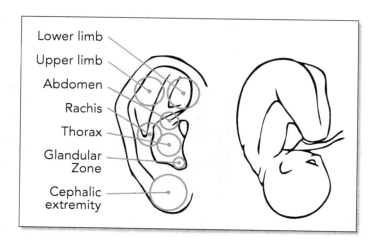

The same spiral principle is true for alternate realities. Each alternate reality is a location within a spiral revolving around a central vortex of stillness which connects with the Universal Energy Field. In many instances it may be more effective to work in an alternate reality to effect healing than in normal reality. This is not any different than a reflexologist touching points on the feet to affect healing within the whole body. Everything is connected and spiraling within the Universal Energy Field; therefore, working in an alternate reality will reflex to all realities.

The therapeutic use of alternate realities is often indicated in cases of trauma, abuse, and addiction. In these cases, normal reality is so painful that a person uses trauma, abuse, and addictions as vehicles to transition into an alternate reality to protect himself. The alternate realities one arrives in are often places where it is possible to communicate with wise teachers, light beings, power animals, and experience magical worlds. These realities are often the source for great music, paintings, poetry, and scientific discoveries. Beethoven was beaten repeatedly by his alcoholic father, and afterwards he would walk through the forests in a dreamlike state and hear beautiful music.

During the 1960's the experience of alternate realities was associated with psychedelics such as LSD, mescaline, and psilocybin, as well as marijuana and opiates. These substances were taken as a rebellion against the normal culture of the time. The transition between normal reality and alternate realities after a psychedelic was ingested was called "getting high" and "tripping." The transition back into normal reality was called "crashing." In other words, the transition between realities was not smooth, and the mind and body paid a price. This is because the use of psychedelics, marijuana, or opiates to transition into alternate realties without the proper knowledge and preparation is naïve at best and tragic in many cases. Taking a psychedelic to transition between realities is like hitting someone with a club to get them to see something different. Sometimes it may work, but at what price?

I know something of the price having worked in psychiatric hospitals from 1969–1977 where I observed the physical and mental effects of hundreds of bad trips. I learned that when alternate realities are associated with psychedelics, marijuana, or opiates, the mind becomes limited in its ability to transition which is a form of dependency. *The Teachings of Don Juan*[2] by Carlos Castaneda illustrates this point very well. Carlos Castaneda, an anthropologist studying indigenous plant healing, apprenticed with a Yacci shaman named Don Juan. In the beginning of his apprenticeship, Don Juan used psychedelic plants to initiate Carlos Castaneda into the sorcerer's world. Later in his apprenticeship, Don Juan told Carlos that it was not necessary to ingest the plants to obtain altered states. He chose the plant route because Carlos was dense and needed to have his world shaken up. From that point on Carlos Castaneda never ingested another psychedelic plant, yet his amazing altered state experiences continued.

It is important when working with people who have learned about alternate realities by taking drugs, or having experienced abuse, addictions, and trauma, to honor their alternate reality experiences and then teach them other methods of transitioning, such as tuning forks. In other words, the problem is not the alternate reality but with the method of transition. Too often, the alternate reality is dismissed as not real and seen as a contributor to an addiction and escape from abuse and trauma. The focus is on stopping the method of transition rather then finding a better method to get there. When a method of transition is stopped without a better method to replace it, the person just seeks out another method which may or may not be better.

The twelve step program has been used effectively for over fifty years to treat addictions. The first step says, "We admitted we were powerless over addiction, i.e., alcohol, gambling, drugs, and that our lives had become unmanageable." This

---

[2] Carlos Castaneda. *Tales of Power.* New York: Simon & Schuster, 1971.

step tells us that the method of transition, i.e., drugs, is no longer working in resonance with our whole life.

The second step says, "We came to believe that a Power greater than ourselves could restore us to sanity." This step tells us that reality is far greater than our current view of reality and that we can have access to a larger reality by letting go of our current method of transition. The only way to let go is trust. Trust is difficult because it appears as though the alternate reality that has been a sanctuary for so long will be lost.

The third step says, "We made a decision to turn our will and our lives over to the care of God as we understood Him." This step surrenders the creation of a new method of transition to the Universal Energy Field. When the field becomes available, transition from one reality to another is as easy as driving from one location to another. With the power of the field, it is just a matter of having the right thought and the energy will follow. The Tai Chi classics say that "thought leads energy."

The Fibonacci tuning forks are "sonic thoughts" that are in precise alignment with the Universal Energy Field. From a twelve step perspective, the sounds of the tuning forks awaken new neural pathways that lead one to a higher power. Each interval of the Fibonacci tuning forks is a turn of the spiral that activates new realities that resonate with their frequency. Once the person realizes that alternate realities are available through sound, it is easier to let go of the cycle of trauma, abuse, and drugs. It is not uncommon to hear alcoholic patients say after a Fibonacci sound treatment that it was "better than drinking." Or to hear drug addicts say, "Wow, that was some high."

I once worked with a heroin addict using tuning forks combined with ear acupuncture. He came once a day for treatments. One day he came up off the table shaking. I asked him what happened. He said that he realized he hadn't taken heroin for two weeks, and that scared him. I thought it was amazing that he just stopped without any withdrawal because the realities he was experiencing via the sound and acupuncture treatments were meeting his needs better than heroin.

Alternate Reality Transition

The key to learning how to transition into alternate realities is what consciousness researchers call *set, setting*, and *method*. *Set* is the first principle of transition and refers to the mental and physical preparation necessary to transition to an alternate reality. *Setting* is the second principle of alternate reality transition and refers to the right environment for transition. *Method* is the third principle of alternate reality transition and refers to the method of transition, i.e., Fibonacci tuning forks.

SET

Set begins with understanding the purpose for transition. Understanding purpose sets a mental tone that resonates with a congruent alternate reality. Some examples of healing/well being purposes might be:

- to enhance creativity
- to discover the source of a disease in order to make changes
- to improve a relationship
- to enhance dreaming
- to heal an addiction
- to heal a trauma
- to become a better athlete
- to discover new ideas for solving a problem

Compare these positive outcome purposes with that of "to get high." Although it can be argued that "getting high" is a form of recreation, the problem is that "getting high" is not clearly defined. Why would one want to get high? If getting high is for recreation, then the proper purpose would be to take a vacation for rest and relaxation. Transitioning with the purpose of "getting high" is like spinning a roulette wheel and hoping for a positive outcome. For example, if the person transitioning has an unconscious unresolved conflict, it may appear in an alternate reality and overwhelm his defenses. This is what was called a "bad trip" in the 1960's.

The physical part of *set* requires that the body be relaxed. The more consciousness and systematic the relaxation, the better. The idea of relaxation resonates with the interval of a Perfect Fifth and is discussed in depth in the chapter on Ideal Nervous System Tuning. The primary reason for being relaxed is simple. Imagine going to a concert after a day of stress without being able to relax and let go. The music has the potential to take you to wonderful places, but you cannot go because your body is locked into the reality of stress. The more you are able to relax and let go, the more you are able to allow the sound to take you places.

In ancient cultures, the body was prepared for transitional experience by taking therapeutic baths, applying essential oils, gentle exercise, neutral music, good food, and a regular pattern of waking and sleeping. These methods still work today. We call them the spa experience or a retreat experience. Our modern day spas are based on the nature cure spas of Europe which have their roots in the dream temples of ancient Greece. Today, the purpose of the spa experience is to take a vacation; it is a time for rest and relaxation. However, in ancient cultures, the spa experience was a preparation for healing by exploring alternate realities.

SETTING

The main requirement for a *setting* is a safe environment. This may be a special room in your home, a healer's office, a church, a temple, or a quiet secluded place in nature. You may be alone, or you may be with others. If you are with others, make sure you trust them and they are congruent with your intentions. If you are working with a healer, make sure the healer understands and supports your transition.

The holy men of the Far East, the priests of ancient Greece, and indigenous shamans from around the world, understand the importance of a safe environment. The ancient Greeks knew that sound had the power to alter consciousness, and listeners were supervised by initiated priests and priestesses who knew the importance of proper guidance. In ancient Greece, music was played using lyres tuned to the same Pythagorean intervals as modern BioSonic tuning forks. Greek lyres were played in temples which were designed with the same Pythagorean intervals used to tune the lyre. The following diagram demonstrates in wave form the musical intervals of the Athena temple of Priene (4th century B.C.).

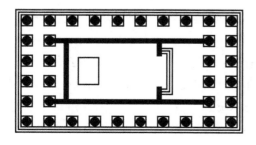 

Notice how the temple architecture creates within it a golden mean spiral which is the basis for the exploration of consciousness using Fibonacci tuning forks.

The Greeks visited these temples for healing and entering into higher states of consciousness to commune with gods and goddesses. When they listened to the sound of the lyre within the temple, the resonance between the listener and temple architecture created the space to transport them into alternate realities.

The great churches of Europe were built according to musical proportions. The intervals of Gregorian chants, based on Pythagorean tunings, were sung in churches whose architectural proportions were the same as the musical intervals of the chants. The sounds of the Gregorian chants, combined with the musical architecture of the church, created a resonant environment for healing. Like tuning forks, they led people to higher states of consciousness.

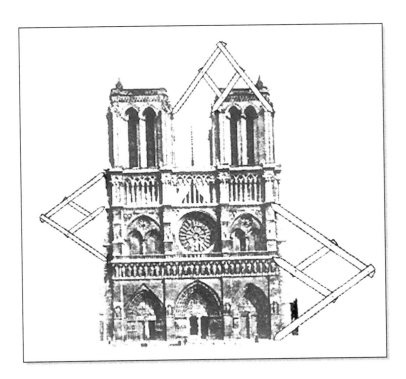

Shamans or healers from indigenous cultures around the world understand the power of the right environment. An accomplished shaman spends hours, even days, preparing the right environment for people to enter into altered states of consciousness. When everything is just right, he uses the sounds of the rhythms of drums, rattles, and whistles like tuning forks. The people experiencing the sha-manic trance speak of a waking dream where they journey to different worlds, talk with wise beings, meet power animals, and reintegrate disassociated parts of their souls.

METHOD

Method is the way we get there—transition. Sound has been used to help people transition into other realities for thousands of years in many different forms which include mantras, drumming, music, chanting, whistles, and singing bowls. The Pythagorean and Fibonacci tuning forks are a modern addition to that long tradi-tion. Here is how the Fibonacci tuning forks work.

The best way to understand the Fibonacci tuning forks is to experience each interval and explore its effects. The first four Fibonacci tuning forks, unison (1/1), octave (1/2), fifth (2/3), and sixth (3/5), are Pythagorean intervals which are part of the Solar Harmonic Spectrum. The next four Fibonacci tuning forks are congruent with Pythagorean tuning but are not traditional musical intervals. Since they are not normal musical tones, they are given only ratio designations. They are 5/8, 8/13, 13/21, and 21/34.

First, lay out the Fibonacci tuning forks in the following order. If you have a Solar Harmonic Set you only need the last four Fibonacci tuning forks. The equivalents between the Solar Harmonic Set and the Fibonacci tuning forks are given in the table.

Fibonacci Tuning Fork	1/1	1/2	2/3	3/5	5/8	8/13	13/21	21/34
Solar Harmonic equivalent	C256	C512	G384	A426.7	No equivalent			

Once you have correctly laid out the Fibonacci tuning forks, the next step is to create the interval(s) you want to work with. The best way to use the Fibonacci tuning forks is to hold three or more in one hand and tap them with the 1/1 (C) tuning fork. This amplifies the beat frequencies or differences between them and creates a "seashell effect." The beat frequencies are what at attracts our hearing into different levels of the spiral through entrainment of different brain centers. If you want to meditate on different Fibonacci intervals using the knee tap technique, you should realize that the Fibonacci tuning forks are tuned very close together. Therefore, the differences between the tones are sometimes challenging to hear when using the knee tap technique to isolate one interval. However, it is also possible to meditate on a single Fibonacci interval as long as it is understood that it takes some practice to hear the difference beats. And even if you do not consciously hear them they are still happening.

Alchemy of Sound
EXPLORING THE FIBONACCI INTERVALS

The following description of the Fibonacci intervals, based on the ascent of consciousness along the pituitary pineal axis, is called the Alchemy of Sound. The different centers along the pituitary pineal axis were called brain stars by Paracelsus, the Swiss physician and alchemist, who was the grandfather of modern medicine. The activation of brain stars is associated with inner voices, light beings, angels, divas, and magical alternate realities.

Modern molecular research may be related to the brain stars of Paracelsus through the activation of endogenous opiate, cannabinoid, and tryptamine molecules. These molecules have long been associated with altered states of consciousness, dreaming, and near-death experiences. Opiate molecules, known as endorphins, are responsible for an inner calm, sometimes called runner's high, that is experienced by athletes. Cannabinoid molecules are termed anandamide which comes from the Sanskrit term "anada" which means bliss. Tryptamine molecules include melatonin, the molecule of dreams, and ayahuasca, which is used by South American Shamans to induce altered states. The Alchemy of Sound views these molecules as naturally occurring, i.e., made within our own body, as part of a gestalt of *set, setting,* and *method.* They are markers of different states of consciousness.

It is said that when you are ready, the teacher appears. In this case, the vehicle is the sound, and within the sound the voice of the teacher is heard.

0 UNIVERSAL ENERGY FIELD OR ZERO POINT

The series begins with 0 which represents nothing or energy without form. Zero is the Unknowable, before the Universal Energy Field which is the source of everything and yet is nothing. 0 is the center of the spiral. It is the beginning and the end, the Alpha and the Omega. In the healing arts, 0 is a still point which functions as a conduit for the Universal Energy Field.

"Be Still and Ye Shall Know"   — 23rd Psalm

1/1

The next step is 1/1 which is the fundamental or the beginning. 1/1 is not an interval because it is "one" and cannot be divided further. 1/1 represents the Universal Energy Field arising from the "no-thingness" of 0.

"In the Beginning was the Word, and the Word was with God,
and the Word was God."   — John 1:1

1/2

The first interval is 1/2 which sounds the octave. The ancient Greeks called the octave *diapason* which means through all possibilities or the space for everything. In terms of the ascent of consciousness 1/2 represents the space within the whole cranium. When tuning forks are sounded, they resonate within the cranium the way a Gregorian chant resonates through a church.

2/3 BALANCE

The next interval is 2/3, the Perfect Fifth, which is the ideal balance between heaven and earth. Lao Tzu wrote: "One has produced Two, Two has produced Three." One of his commentators explains, "These words mean that One has been divided into Yin, the female Principle, and Yang, the male principle. These two have joined, and of their junction came the harmony of Three. The spirit of Three, condensing, has produced all beings (realities)."[3]

---

[3] Lao Tsu. *Tao Te Ching.* New York: Vintage Books, 1972.

The interval of a fifth causes the sphenoid bone to vibrate and move in harmonic patterns. The sphenoid looks like a butterfly with its greater and lesser wings, and the pterygoid processes look like the "feet" of the a butterfly ready to land on a flower. The sphenoid moves and rotates in different directions. If we could see the sphenoid moving, it would look like a great bird flying through the sky and navigating different wind currents.

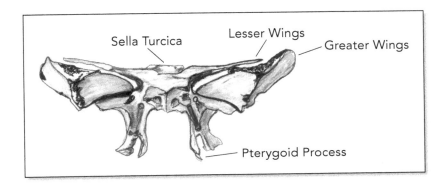

The superior center of the sphenoid bone is called the sella turcica which means Turkish Saddle. The sella turcica is located in the center of the forehead just above the eyes and is oftentimes referred to in consciousness literature as the Seat of the Third Eye. The sella turcica has four posts to which the diaphragm sella is attached. The diaphragm sella is stretched between the posts like a finely tuned drumhead and is very sensitive to vibration.

The pituitary gland sits on top of the diaphragm sella. When the vibrations of the Perfect Fifth stimulate sphenoid movements, the diaphragm sella resonates in harmony. Simultaneously, the pituitary gland releases endogenous opiates which are the precursors to the release of nitric oxide. The opiates free consciousness from being concerned with the body and daily activities by its sedating effect, leading us to greater feelings of well-being. The nitric oxide release catalyzes the body to heal, detoxify, and, in general, take care of itself. This allows our conscious awareness to move into higher states.

The pituitary gland and the diaphragm sella can be symbolized by the archetypal image of Aladdin flying on his magic carpet. When we are in optimal health and well-being, the sphenoid is like a magic carpet with wings that glide effortlessly through the energy currents of life into the higher realms of consciousness. The pituitary gland, at the center of the sphenoid, sits in a highly-balanced still point vortex. Dr. Randolph Stone writes about obtaining this state of balance in his *Advanced Polarity Therapy* notes.

"When the mind is stilled here, it is called RUH or the sanctuary of Rest by being still. Here is the tabernacle of God in man as his mountain of inspiration and revelation from higher regions. All saints, saviors and prophets have used this highway to the spiritual regions. This is the sanctuary and magic mirror where higher creations can be seen and traveled in on the sound current. This center was also mentioned in Arabian nights as the Aladdin's Lamp found by great effort and many trials."[4]

3/5 DREAMS

The ba, a form of spirit, is represented as a jabiru-bird
which leaves the body during dreams and death.

(Egypt, 3rd–1st century B.C., Ny Carlsberg Glyptothek, Copenhagen)

The next interval in the Fibonacci Series is 3/5 which is the interval of a 6th. The 3/5 interval is the beginning of ascent into higher spiritual levels. It can be visualized in many ways. The psychic, Edgar Cayce, called it the interval of the mystic fire. Its archetype is the first step of Alice into the rabbit hole on the way to Wonderland. The alchemists knew it as the interval of ascension and visualized it as the image of a phoenix rising.

When our consciousness is located at the sella turcica and optimal sphenoid balance is obtained, our life energy spontaneously lifts up within a vortex of energy into the third ventricle of the brain. The third ventricle of the brain is known in Sanskrit literature as the Cave of Brahma in which is located the seat of resonance with the ocean of cosmic vibrations. The archetype of the ascent of consciousness into the third ventricle is seen in the image of a unicorn spreading its wings. The unicorn's wings symbolize a balanced sphenoid, and its horn represents the third

---

[4] Dr. Randolph Stone. *Polarity Therapy: The Complete Works. Vol II. Vitality Balance.* Reno, NV: CRCS Publications, 1987, p. 189.

eye. The unicorn lifts up on its journey across the rainbow bridge through many realities in order to reach the pot of gold. The alchemists symbolized the pot of gold as the Philosopher's Stone. Today we call it the Universal Energy Field.

When our consciousness enters the third ventricle of the brain, anandamide molecules are released. The appearance of these molecules signifies that our consciousness has left normal reality and has entered a dream state. Many American Indian tribes refer to the third ventricle as the Dream Lodge where their ancestors sat in Council and advised them on alternate pathways of vision. Psychics and seers call the third ventricle the region of a thousand lights that intertwine to create dreams within dreams.

5/8 CAVE OF WHISPERS

When our consciousness continues to rise, it moves us further into the Cave of Brahma (the third ventricle of the brain). The thousand lights are still available; however, we are drawn to inner voices as we let go of thoughts that are no longer necessary. The inner voices are known as the thousand whispers of Brahma. It is here we discover our inner voice, voice of wisdom, inner guidance, and the healer within. The information we need to obtain a sense of balance and peace by taking correct action becomes available to us.

When we listen to our inner voice, the vibration of wisdom resonates throughout the cave of Brahma. This, in turn, vibrates the diaphragm stelle and oscillates the pituitary gland on its anterior and posterior lobes causing it to release a sequence of hormones in alignment with the wisdom teachings. Concurrently, the sphenoid bone vibrates and moves into a new pattern. The temporal bones glide into a new receiving position, making the bones available for the input from normal reality.

While our consciousness is in the Cave of Brahma (the third ventricle of the brain), it is surrounded by cerebrospinal fluid (CSF). Alchemically, CSF is mercurial in nature and is called the Dew from Heaven, Divine Water, the Fountain of Youth, and/or quicksilver. Anatomically, it is transparent, slightly yellowish, consisting of saline or a salt water liquid. It is secreted in the third ventricle by the choroid plexus which is located on the walls of the ventricle. They drip CSF into the ventricle the same way moisture will collect in a cave.

When we listen to the voice of wisdom, the CSF is simultaneously encoded with the vibrational essence of the dialogue. Many healing arts practitioners who work with CSF talk about their experiences with the intelligence of this fluid.

Dr. Andrew Still, D.O., the founder of Osteopathic Medicine said:

> "Cerebrospinal fluid is the highest known element in the human body... He who is able to reason will see that this great river of life must be tapped and the withering field irrigated at once or the harvest of health is forever lost."[5]

The cerebrospinal fluid carries within it the essence of our inner wisdom and communicates this to the rest of our body. It flows out of the third ventricle, down the cerebral aqueduct, and into the fourth ventricle. The fourth ventricle represents the transition from super-consciousness into somatic or body consciousness. Energetically, the Egyptians called it the Ankh, where energy makes its way from the divine into normal conscious reality.

From the fourth ventricle, the CSF spirals down through the central canal of the spinal cord, where it energetically encodes each chakra with its role in the wisdom teaching. The CSF is stored in a reservoir at the base of the sacrum where it is known as the sleeping Kundalini Force.

> The Kundalini is sleeping because it is encoded with wisdom that has not been acted upon.

It is potential that needs a spark to set it in motion. That spark can be something in our life, either positive or negative, which brings us the motivation to act. When the Kundalini awakens, it rises with intense struggle. Each step of the way, the elemental energy of the chakras is manifested and balanced again and again until normal reality resonates with the message of the wisdom voices.

---

[5] Dr. Andrew Taylor Still. *Philosophy of Osteopathy*. Indianapolis, IN: The American Academy of Osteopathy, 1986.

8/13 MYSTICAL PASSAGEWAY

For our consciousness to rise higher, it must pass through the Mystical Passageway, which is also known as the Hidden Mountain Pass, the Crystal Door, or the Magic Mirror. The Mystical Passageway is located at the posterior superior portion of the third ventricle directly below the pineal gland. Discovering and passing through the Mystical Passageway takes us beyond the voices of wisdom and closer to their source.

Discovering and passing through the Mystical Passageway requires you to honor the voices of wisdom. The process of honoring is one of acting on the encoded wisdom messages stored in the sacrum or sacred bone. A fundamental principle of Alchemy found in the Emerald Tablets of Hermes is "As Above, So Below." This means that spiritual reality (above) must be in resonance with normal reality (below). The same principle is found in the Lord's Prayer: Our Father whom art in Heaven hallowed be thy name. Thy will be done on Earth (below, normal reality) as in Heaven (above, spiritual reality).

When normal reality is not congruent with spiritual reality, a state of life dissonance results. Resolving life dissonances means that we must do the work to bring our normal reality into alignment with vision. The act of doing the work in order to come into alignment with the wisdom voices is to manifest our vision. The work creates an inner heat which is known by many names including Tumo, the Sacred Fire, the Fire of Shiva, and the Alchemic Furnace. True inner heat is a heat that warms the cerebrospinal fluid throughout the whole body and specifically in the third ventricle where it becomes a warm mist of CSF that rises up and through the Mystical Passageway.

13/21 THE GREAT DIVIDE

Anatomically our consciousness comes to a soft tissue seat much like the sella turcica that supports the auditory and visual colliculi. These are small mounds of specialized brain tissue that receive visual and auditory energy signals from our normal reality through our eyes and ears where it is then directed to other areas of our brain. It is information that is normally interpreted into the fabric of everyday reality.

The center point of the criss-crossing auditory and visual data is directly below the pineal gland. Flowing between the soft tissue seat of the auditory and visual colliculi is a river of cerebrospinal fluid which connects the right and left hemispheres of the brain. In order to cross the river of CSF we must be in perfect balance. Virgo is the astrological archetype for the state of perfect balance necessary to ascend to higher states of consciousness. Virgo is the astrological sign of perfection which is both ruled and exalted by Mercury.

In the alchemical drawing below, the feet of Mercury stand in perfect balance (Virgo) on the wings of the sphenoid. The body of Mercury represents the third ventricle and the two fighting figures represent the lateral ventricles and the struggle necessary to raise the Kundalini. Mercury holds a staff of Caduceus in each hand which represents the mercurial principle.

Simultaneously, Mercury spreads new wings which represent the seat of balance located at the soft tissue seat of the auditory and visual colliculi. The crown represents the pineal gland and the three principles of wave, pulse, and form which are also portrayed as the sun, moon, and the symbol of mercury on top of the center of the crown. The mercury symbol represents the exaltation of Mercury in Virgo. It is the "key" and passageway to the Universal Energy Field or what the alchemists called the Philosopher's Stone.

When we are in perfect balance between heaven and earth, the waters part and we can ascend. This is the Archetype of Moses parting the waters in order for the Jews to reach the promised land. If something is out of balance or when the

An alchemical representation of the ventricular system
according to F. Basilius Valentinus

message of the wisdom teachings are not being acted upon, our consciousness can fall into the river of CSF. We must return to normal reality to do more work. However, when perfect balance is obtained, consciousness sits in deep reverent stillness within the cathedral of the cranium and before the Gateway of Heaven waiting to enter the pineal gland or the Eye of God.

The German earth scientist and naturalist, Victor Schauberger, gives an insight into how this happens. He visited the salmon streams of Washington State in the 1930's to investigate how salmon were able to swim upstream against a strong current. He was especially interested in how they were able to negotiate waterfalls. Schauberger discovered that water coming over the falls created natural spirals, much like water going down a drain. The merging of these spirals created water cyclones. The salmon struggled against the current to come to a place of perfect balance within the water, and just at the right moment they were pulled up over the waterfall within the vortex of the spirals. Schauberger believed that the energy within the vortex levitated the salmon to the top of the waterfalls. In a similar way, when we come to an optimal state of balance between heaven and earth, our consciousness is lifted into higher realms across what seemed like an impossible leap, within a vortex of stillness.

21/34 THE EYE OF GOD

The pineal gland is named from the Latin *pinus* which means pine cone. It is unique because it sits alone in the upper center of the brain just above the third ventricle. Every site in our brain has a left and right counterpart, i.e., two eyes, two ears, two nostrils, except for the pineal gland. The pineal gland becomes visible in the developing fetus at seven weeks which is exactly the time male or female gender can be seen. It develops from specialized tissues in the roof of the mouth and migrates through the third ventricle to the center of the brain. Here it is surrounded by our limbic brain which consists of structures involved in the experience of emotions such as joy, rage, fear, anxiety, and pleasure.

As an archetype, the pineal functions by overseeing and integrating all the realms of dualities. When consciousness enters the pineal gland, it transcends duality and travels on the Great Dream Highway to the higher realms of energy and spiritual realities. It is here that great truths are instantly understood, and the vibratory nature of reality is revealed. The higher spiritual reason behind a question, thought, or challenge which began in normal reality is illuminated, and we know, with crystal clarity, all the connections from above to below.

When the waters part and our consciousness crosses the great divide, the pineal gland releases a molecule called melatonin. Melatonin is a tryptamine molecule, and is in the family of molecules associated with psychedelics. It serves as an antioxidant as well as a regulator of our body's time clock. It is very effective in cases of jet lag and in helping you to sleep on a more regular schedule. In many ways, melatonin serves a similar purpose as the release of opiates by the pituitary, which is to create a state of balanced state of calmness allowing our consciousness to ascend into the mysteries of the pineal gland.

When our consciousness ascends, the pineal gland vibrates like a tuning fork. It is believed that the vibrating pineal gland secretes endogenous molecules similar to ayahuasca, LSD, mesculin, and psilocybin, all of which are from the tryptamine family. The best known of the tryptamine molecules are LSD, psilocybin which is the active ingredient of "magic mushrooms," and DMT which is the active ingredient of ayahuasca, which is used by the shamans of South America.

Mystics talk about experiencing a "whirring" sound associated with the pineal gland as they enter into higher states of consciousness. Many people who have had a near death experience report a similar whirring sound preceding a tunnel of light. The sound resonates through our cranial cavity in much the same way as an orchestra resonates in a concert hall. When we leave still point within our pineal fland, our consciousness vibrates with spiritual sound. We enter into a spiritual journey and are guided by higher intelligences to experience what we need to learn.

While our consciousness is traveling the Rainbow Bridge, the vibrations of our experiences are resonating throughout our cranium. The pineal gland then becomes like a tuning fork sympathetically vibrating the stream of CSF and sending spiritual potentized water, called the Dew from Heaven, throughout our CSF network. Simultaneously, our cranial bones are oscillating in new patterns, and our visual and auditory nerves via our auditory and visual colliculi are seeing and hearing a new spiritual reality.

Overtone Tuning Forks

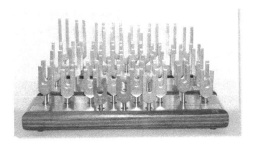

Playing, singing, and listening to overtones has long been a method of healing and spiritual awakening. Buddhist chanters in Mongolia and Tibet sang overtones which were embedded with sacred mantras. While they chanted, these mantras would resonate overtone sounds in their sinus cavities and spaces within their cranium. The result was both beautiful and powerful in its healing and spiritual effect. Many cultures have produced bowls, that when tapped or rubbed, produce different overtones. The most well-known bowls that do this are the Tibetan Singing Bowls. These bowls come in different sizes and are made from seven different metals. When the bowls are played, they produce overtones that vibrate the different metals. The effect of overtones resonating with different metals creates a pulsation between heaven and earth.

One of the more interesting overtone instruments used by shamans are pre-Columbian double chambered whistling vessels known simply as Peruvian Whistling Vessels. These vessels were discovered in graves throughout Peru and Northern Mexico. They are still used by shamans to induce altered states of consciousness. Each whistling vessel has a different high-pitched tuning. When seven Peruvian Whistling Vessels are continuously sounded, they create thousands of overtones.

When the listener is immersed in these overtones, a cascade of structural and physiological events occur in the body. When investigating the high-pitched overtone sounds of Peruvian Whistling Vessels, physiologists at the Franklyn Institute in Germany reported definitive bodily changes in heart rate, blood pressure, respiration, and basal metabolism. It is also believed that the small intervallic gaps between the overtones cause a change in the distance between neural synaptic junctions. This change results in a release of endorphins, beta canaboids, and DMT molecules in the synaptic gap.

The Russian composer, Alexander Scriaben, in the early 1900's believed that sounding overtones would bring forth a new era and unite Heaven and Earth. His last composition, *Mysterium*, was to be played in India using etheric bells hung from clouds that sounded very high-pitched overtones like wind chimes. Scriaben visualized himself sitting on earth listening to overtone voices of Devas, or Spirit Angels, that would bring forth a new era of enlightenment.

Musically, overtones are a series of tones starting from a fundamental tone and ascending infinitely in pitch. The overtone series ascends in whole numbers 1, 2, 3, 4, 5, 6, 7, 8, 9............n with 1:1 being the fundamental or first tone. The relationship between the numbers of the overtone series forms the basis of Pythagorean musical intervals and an infinite number of other intervals. For example, the next interval after the fundamental is 1:2, an octave. The next interval is 2:3, a fifth which is followed by 3:4 which is the interval of a fourth.

The Solar Harmonic Spectrum, Otto Tuners, and Angel Tuners are all tuned to a fundamental frequency of 8 cps. The primary reason for 8 cps is based on the Schuman Resonance. In 1957, W. O. Schuman calculated the Earth-ionosphere cavity resonance frequencies, which are named for him as the Schuman resonance. The Schuman Resonance consists of naturally occurring electromagnetic signals which circulate and pulsate between the earth and the ionosphere at approximately 7.7–8 cps. The Schuman Resonance is thought by many to be the "heart beat" of planet earth and fundamental to the healing process.

The 8 cps fundamental also gives rise to some interesting speculation. When the Schuman Resonance was first discovered, it was 7.5 Hz and has been gradually rising. Many speculate this increasing pulse is signaling a shift in consciousness. The 8 cps fundamental is designed to entrain the Schuman Resonance as well as support our transformation into higher states of consciousness.

Another reason why the number 8 was chosen was because in the ancient art of numerology, the number 8 symbolizes the integration of Heaven, the top circle of the 8, and Earth, the bottom circle of the 8. The point that the circles cross is in the center and represents a still point between Heaven and Earth. The number 8 turned on its side is the sign of infinity, or a place of perfect balance between polarities.

The following table begins with an 8 cps fundamental which is doubled 9 octaves to 4096 cps. Tuning forks are shown with the octaves they resonate.

8 cps	Fundamental Tone
16 cps	
32 cps	Otto Tuner 32™
64 cps	Otto Tuner 64™
128 cps	Otto Tuner 128™
256 cps	Lower C of Solar Harmonic Spectrum™
512 cps	Upper C of Solar Harmonic Spectrum™
1024 cps	
2048 cps	
4096 cps	Crystal Tuner™

The image of Jacob's Ladder is often associated with the overtone series and ascension of overtones. Jacob's Ladder begins on Earth and rises to Heaven. Earth is a metaphor for the fundamental tone and each step of the ladder represents a different overtone ascending to Heaven. The ancient scholars of the Kabbalah believed that angels lived in the spaces known as intervals between the ascending overtones. These intervalic spaces between overtones were known by the ancient Taoists as the Mysterious Mountain Passageways leading to angelic kingdoms.

When the overtone tuning forks are sounded, they create a very high pitch, much like the sound of dolphins or whales. The interaction between the different overtone tuning forks creates pulsations which sonically massage the listener by creating an ever changing environment of sound waves. The pulsating quality of the upper over-tones resonates the bone structures of the cranium like the sounding board of a piano. This resonance unwinds cranial sutures and allows increased cranial bone movement creating a deep internal resonance in the intradural cranial membranes. When we listen to the overtones, a cascade of structural and physiological events occurs in our body. The sound waves spread through our brain causing millions of neural synaptic junctions to seek out resonance with the different intervalic overtone relationships.

When we listen to the overtones, it is common for us to experience an increased inner heat. This happens because of the increased cranial movement which directly affects our centers of metabolism and increases our blood flow. In mystical terms, the inner heat is called the fire of transformation which is known as Tumo, the Fire of Shiva, or the Alchemic Furnace. It is believed that this inner heat has the ability to burn away our karma and transmute our physical form into pure spirit. The Himalayan saints sit in the high cold mountains of India dressed only in loin cloths. The Tumo heat from their bodies, caused by the burning of karma, upholds the Dharma of the universe and melts the snow and ice around them into puddles of clear water.

Each overtone and combination of overtones are bands of frequencies. These frequency bands are resonant with different areas of our mind, emotions, and bodies. We need access to all of our resources on a vibrational level. If we delete a range of frequencies, this can show up in many ways in our daily life. It may appear as a repeating behavior pattern, disease, depression, or a general lack of wellness. A radio station is a good example of the effects of frequencies. A radio station broadcasts lots of information over a frequency band. If that band is compromised, then the information is corrupted with static and is not available.

Angel Tuners™

The Angel Tuners consist of three overtone tuning forks tuned at 4121 cps, 4096 cps, and 4200 cps. When sounding the Angel Tuner overtone tuning forks, the 4096 tuning fork is held in the right hand and the other two are held in the left hand. The 4096 tuning fork is tapped against the other two tuning forks in the left hand.

Crystal Tuner™

The Crystal Tuner is a 4096 cps tuning fork and the main tuning fork in the set of three ninth octave overtone tuning forks called Angel Tuners. The Crystal Tuner is tuned to the 9th octave of the overtone series, which is said to open the doorway to the angelic kingdoms and

to an 8 cps fundamental tone, which is the heart tone of the planet Earth. When the crystal tuner is tapped on the back side of the quartz crystal, it sets the crystal into vibration.

Chakra Tuning

The Crystal Tuner is a powerful sonic instrument for tuning chakras. The oscillating quartz crystal emits a full spectrum of light which is amplified by the pulse between the Crystal Tuner and the quartz crystal. When the mind is focused on the color combinations which are used to activate a chakra for color healing, the colors are channeled through the point of the quartz crystal to the area to be healed. Here is how it works.

Hold the quartz crystal in your left or right hand between the thumb and fingers. Point the quartz crystal to the chakra or chakras to be activated. To evaluate the chakras, it would be helpful to read the chapter on Tuning Forks and The Five Elements. Hold the Crystal Tuner by its handle with the other hand. Gently tap one or more times on the rough end of the crystal (not on the tip) with the flat side of the Crystal Tuner.

Cleaning Crystals

Quartz crystals absorb and channel energy. They need to be cleaned from time to time in order to function at their maximum capacity. Cleaning a quartz crystal with the Crystal Tuner is easy. Hold the quartz crystal in your left or right hand between the thumb and fingers. Hold the Crystal Tuner by its handle with the other hand. Gently tap on the rough end of the crystal (not on the tip) with the flat side of the Crystal Tuner one or more times. The Crystal Tuner will sound, and the quartz crystal will come to life.

Next, move the flat side of the Crystal Tuner along the side of the crystal like you are patting it. Always move the Crystal Tuner from the back or rough edge of the crystal to the point. Move the tuning fork slowly, and as you pass the point, allow the Crystal Tuner to sweep outwards and visualize any excess accumulated energy returning to the light. Do this with each side of the crystal one or more times. The same method will work to clear other stones such as diamonds, emeralds, amethysts, jade, onyx, rubies, etc.

Space Clearing

FENG SHUI WITH TUNING FORKS

Space clearing is clearing rooms of unwanted energy that can lead to clutter, poor thought processes, confusion, or feelings of being overwhelmed, all of which reduce available life energy. Space clearing with a Crystal Tuner can be done in any room of the house to balance energy. The Crystal Tuner can be used to clear healing rooms, meditation rooms, studios, or when traveling to clear hotel or motel rooms. Any space is suitable for clearing with a Crystal Tuner.

Hold the quartz crystal in your left or right hand between the thumb and fingers. Hold the Crystal Tuner by its handle with the other hand. Gently tap on the rough end of the crystal (not on the tip) with the flat side of the Crystal Tuner one or more times. The Crystal Tuner will sound, and the quartz crystal will come to life. Keep your hands about 18 inches apart and reach out towards the space you want to clear with both hands. Allow the energy to flow between the crystal and Crystal Tuner and also flow out into the space. Sense the energy move out into the room on waves of sound, like water moving away from a pebble into a pond. Envision a receptacle, such as a trash can or a black hole, filled with white, cleansing light positioned just outside of the space you are clearing. Send the energy into the receptacle. Repeat the process in different corners of the room as needed.

Osteophonic (Otto) Tuning Forks

Osteophonic tuning forks are specially designed with weights placed on the prongs. The weights create a stronger vibration which is transferred through the tuning fork stem directly into tissue. The word Otto is short for osteophonic which means to vibrate bones. One can feel bones and tissue vibrate in resonance with an Otto tuning fork when the stem is held to a point on the body. Otto tuning forks can also be used like regular tuning forks to create a pure sound. Otto tuning forks

weights

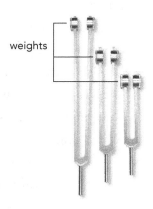

cannot be tapped together to create overtones. Otto tuning forks work best with low pitches and do not work as well with medium to high pitches.

There are three Otto tuning forks called the Otto 32, Otto 64, and Otto 128. The numbers stand for cycles per second.

The Otto 128 is the primary Otto tuning fork which vibrates a Perfect Fifth pulse that can be placed on the body and transmitted directly into joints, bones, tissues, acupuncture points, and trigger points. The Otto 128 cps is based on the difference tone of a Perfect Fifth. For example, C is 256 cps and G is 384 cps. The difference tone is arrived at by subtracting 256 cps from 384 cps which equals 128 cps. This means that when you are listening to a Perfect Fifth you are hearing a 128 cps pulse that is created between the C and G tuning forks. The dynamics of the Perfect Fifth have been discussed in depth in previous chapters.

To sound the Otto 128, hold it by the stem and tap the flat side of the weights on your knees or the palm of your hand.

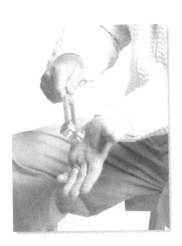

To learn this technique, tap the Otto 128 and press the tuning fork onto one of your knuckles. Make contact with the base of the stem and gently press until you feel the vibration being transferred to your body. Experiment with different pressures—start light and then gradually increase until you feel the maximum vibration.

The method for using an Otto 128 or Otto 64 on a specific point is:

1. Find the exact point using whatever method is appropriate.
2. Place your index finger on the point.

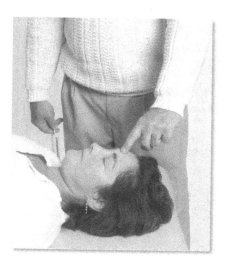

3. Tap the Otto 128 on your knee or palm.

4. Bring the Otto 128 to your index finger and simultaneously slide your index finger away while bringing the base of the tuning fork stem onto the point.

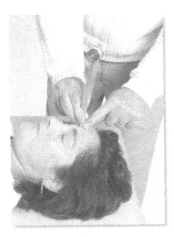

In general, it is always good to place your free hand somewhere else on the body.

> Our research suggests that using the Otto 128 two times on any one point is adequate. The reason is that too much vibration will over stimulate an area and cause a decrease rather than an increase in nitric oxide. So in this case, less is more.

If you have a history of osteoporosis or have a fracture, do not press the Otto 128 to your bones. If you feel any pain when pressing the tuning fork to a bone, do not continue to press. Many EMT's carry an Otto 128 tuning fork to test for bone fractures. The vibration of the fork causes the bone to vibrate. If there is a fracture present, the person will experience pain. It is not as good as an X-ray; however, in the field it gives a very strong indication.

The Otto 128 is a very versatile tuning fork with many applications. The Otto 128 is great for working with joint mobility and stiffness in joints as well as balancing the autonomic nervous system. In general, it can be pressed to any joint. The vibration will effect a spike of nitric oxide in both nerve and vascular tissue which leads to vasodilation, nervous system balance, and an increase in opiate molecules. The result is enhanced circulation and less pain.

General Balance

HEART BALANCE   Place the Otto 128 on your sternum, your chest bone. Feel the vibration and imagine your heart softening. This point spikes nitric oxide and sends a wave throughout the whole body. (Note: Do not use this area if you have a pacemaker.)

THIRD EYE BALANCE   Place the Otto 128 on your third eye—the space between and just above your eyes. Close your eyes and feel the vibration move through your cranium. This point balances the cranial base and enhances sphenoid/occipital movement.

AUTONOMIC NERVOUS SYSTEM BALANCE Place the Otto 128 on your lower sacrum, the bone at the base of your spine. Close your eyes and feel the vibration move through your lower pelvis. This point balances the sympathetic and parasympathetic nervous systems by stimulating the ganglion impar.

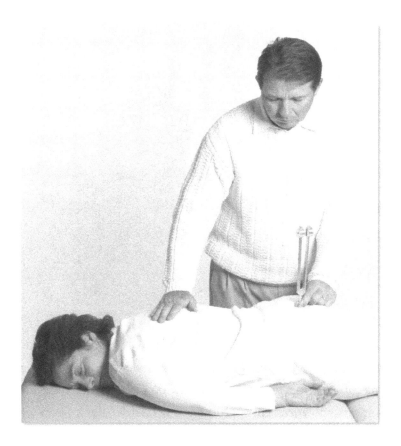

PELVIC BALANCE Place the Otto 128 on the left and right side of your anterior superior iliac spine and feel the vibrations move through your pelvis. This point helps release the psoas muscle allowing the pelvis to open and the organs within the pelvis to relax.

VISION POINT   Place the Otto 128 on the frontal fontanel and sense the vibration moving through your cranium. This point stimulates the pineal gland and visualization.

JOINT BALANCE   The Otto 128 can be used to relax tense tissue around any joint. The Otto 128, because of its ability to spike nitric oxide, is recommended to relieve the symptoms of arthritis. The Otto 128 can be placed anywhere near the joint and the vibrations will travel through the joint. There is not a specific point when working with joints, only the area of the joint.

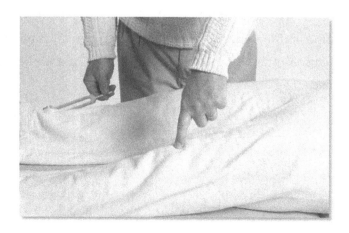

Use your index finger to mark on the joint you want to press.

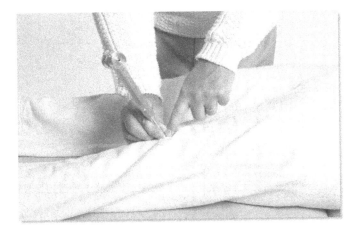

Tap the Otto 128 and press it to the point.

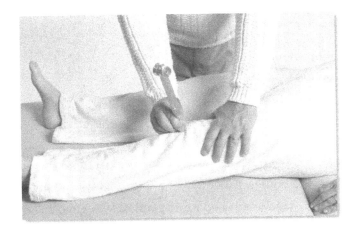

Move your pointing hand to anyplace on the body that seems appropriate.

Otto 128 Points and Protocol Sessions

FIVE STAR BALANCE SESSION PROTOCOL

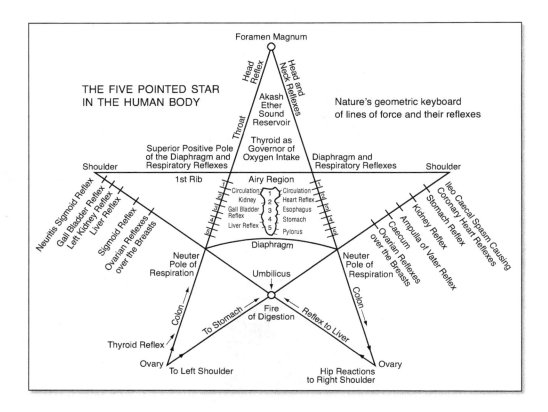

The five star session is a general mind/body balance based on the ratios of a Perfect Fifth overlayed on the bodies structure. The Otto 128 tuning forks can be placed anywhere along the diagonals based on the reflexes. A general session would be as follows.

STEP 1   Place directly on the third eye (glabella) and/or 1 inch below the external occipital protuberance.

STEP 2   Place on the upper left shoulder (scapula acromion). Then place on right side.

STEP 3   Place on the right upper hip (anterior superior iliac crest).

STEP 4   Place on the upper right shoulder (scapula acromion).

STEP 5   Place on the left upper hip (anterior superior iliac crest).

In general, visualize the vibration moving as a wave along the diagonal lines of the five star pattern.

TMJ PROTOCOL

STEP 1   Place on the outer side of the two large muscles of the neck where they join the back of the head.

STEP 2   Place on the temporal bone mastoid process.

STEP 3   Place on the mandible just below TMJ or very lightly directly on TMJ.

The Otto 128 as an Adjunct to Acupuncture, Reflexology, and Trigger Point Therapy

The Otto 128 can sonically stimulate acupuncture points, ear, hand and foot reflex points, and/or trigger points. The use of the Otto 128 with these points requires a knowledge of acupuncture, reflexology and trigger point therapy. However, basic points can be learned from books and used.

Here are my recommendations for books which display points that can be used with your Otto 128:

- Serizawa, Katsusuke. "Vital Points for Oriental Therapy." *Tsubo.* San Francisco, CA: Japan Publications, Inc., 1976.

- Beaulieu John. *Polarity Therapy Workbook.* Stone Ridge, NY: BioSonic Enterprises, 1992.

The Otto 64—Balancing the Autonomic Nervous System

The Otto 64 is a sixty-four cycle per second weighted tuning fork. It is tuned one octave below the Otto 128 and produces a lower tone, which like the Otto 128 vibrates to the pulse of a Perfect Fifth. The Otto 64 is specifically designed to place on and vibrate the sacrum in order to balance the autonomic nervous system. The Otto 128 can also be placed on the sacrum; however, the Otto 64 creates a lower vibration which creates a stronger resonance with the sacrum.

The sacrum, pictured below, is a triangular bone located between the ileums. The small bones at the base of the sacrum are called the coccyx.

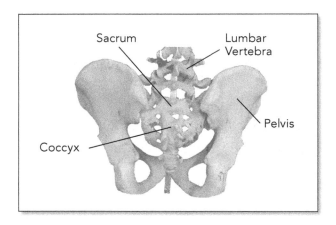

The autonomic nervous system, along with the endocrine system, controls the body's internal organs and regulates many overall body functions such as blood flow, temperature, basal metabolism, muscle tone, and our ability to relax and stay alert and ready for action. The autonomic nervous system is divided into two parts called sympathetic and parasympathetic. Although the relationship between these two aspects of the autonomic nervous system is complex, for our purposes we can look at the interaction in terms of reciprocal interplay.

This means that they act somewhat like a teeter-totter: When the activity of the sympathetic nervous system increases, the activity of the parasympathetic nervous system decreases, and vice versa. Reciprocal interplay is organized by a center in the brain called the hypothalamus. Balanced discharge between sympathetic and parasympathetic is necessary for health and well-being. A loss of balance leads to physical, mental, and emotional imbalances. The nature of these imbalances depends upon the side that is dominant.

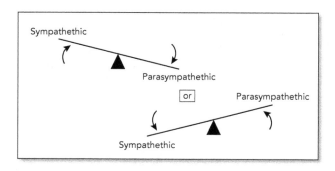

When the Otto 64 is placed on the sacrum, the sacrum acts as a resonator, much like the sounding board of a piano. The sacrum sends the pulse of a fifth into surrounding anatomical structures, muscles, and nerves. The practitioner does not have to press the Otto 64 to a precise point because once the sacrum is set in motion, it acts as a tuning fork by sympathetic resonance.

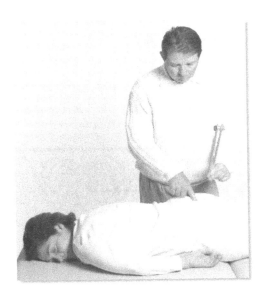 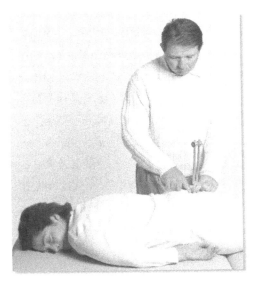

Anatomically, the vibration of the sacrum stimulates the ganglion impar which is located behind the coccyx and has a direct effect on the sympathetic nervous system. Vibrating the sacrum with the Otto 64 resets the autonomic nervous system, similar to a computer reset. When it is stimulated, it causes the autonomic nervous system, to "teeter-totter," go into motion, and come into a state of new balance.

Due to the stresses of living, we are often functioning via the sympathetic nervous system. We are in "fight or flight" response, alert, on the go, and ready to accomplish our goals. In the extreme, the sympathetic nervous system activates to protect us from trauma. Even though the traumatic event may have passed, the sympathetic nervous system maintains a heightened state of alertness. Over time this heightened state can contribute to many physical and mental symptoms including lack of sleep, body aches and pains, depression, sexual dysfunction, menstrual dysfunction for women, and an array of autoimmune and proinflammation disorders.

Energetically, the Otto 64 allows the floor of the pelvis, called the perineum, to relax. The perineum is the anatomical location of the Earth chakra. In astrology, it is associated with the sign of Scorpio. The Scorpion hides underneath rocks in the dark. We suppress our emotions and deepest secrets into the perineal floor, and they are held in place by the earth chakra where the primary emotion is fear. We are afraid to bring them into the light. When they start to emerge too quickly, we either retreat further or "sting."

The Otto 64 allows for a soft shift into the parasympathetic nervous system and does not overwhelm the system or cause a sympathetic response which leads to a further contraction. When the nervous system switches to parasympathetic blood, flow increases to the pelvis region. The result is a deep relaxation and an increased ability to be more receptive.

The word "sacrum" means sacred bone. Since ancient times, the sacrum has been considered a source of power within which lies a coiled snake representing the sleeping force of Kundalini energy.

When the sympathetic and parasympathetic come into balance the Kundalini energy naturally rises. Dr. Stone says in his book, *The Mysterious Sacrum*,

> "When the sleeping force is lifted up to the brain by intense concentration and devotion, the serpent power ascends upward on the tree of life and awakens the latent sleeping force in the pineal gland and unfolds the pattern of cosmic consciousness."[6]

---

[6] Dr. Randolph Stone. *Polarity Therapy: The Complete Works Vol II. The Mysterious Sacrum.* Reno, NV: CRCS Publications 1987, p. 14.

The Otto 32

The Otto 32 tuning fork is a large tuning fork for stimulating and balancing peripheral nerves, lymphatic flow, and cranial suture mobility. The technique for using the Otto 32 is to tap the middle of the tuning fork on the lower part of the hand. This sets the tuning fork in motion, and you can see the weights and prongs moving.

Next, bring the Otto 32 to the area of the body you want to work with and slowly move it just off the skin.

LYMPHATIC SESSION

A lymphatic drainage session can be performed anywhere on the body. It uses flowing watery movement with the Otto 32 in the direction of lymphatic flow.

Begin by holding the Otto 32 just above the skin. Tap the Otto 32 on your hand and move it in the direction of the arrows on the chart. Remember to move it towards the heart. The movement should be slow and like a wave which surges forward and then retreats. You may do a whole body lymph session or work specific areas. If you sense the lymph is stagnant, cold, or moving too slowly, stop, and place the Otto 128 directly on the area. Do not press too deeply, just enough to vibrate the tissues and stimulate the lymph.

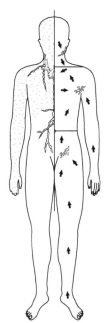

CRANIAL SUTURE SESSION

Cranial bone mobility is very important for general health and well being. The cranial sutures, although believed to be fused in traditional medicine, are thought to maintain movement throughout life in cranial osteopathic medicine. Although the movements are micro-movements they can nevertheless be palpated by trained practitioners. These micro-movements have a lot to do with human tuning. The whole cranium can be imagined as a crystal antenna where each bone can freely move into different positions to receive frequencies.

When cranial bone movement is restricted due to suture holding, many symptoms can result. The founder of Cranial Osteopathy, Dr. William G. Sutherland, created a helmet device that allowed him to restrict the mobility of different cranial bones. He reported experiencing different symptoms from aches and pains in different joints, headaches, depression, and digestive problems. I began my study of cranial therapy with Dr. Arthur Lincoln Pauls, head of the British School of Osteopathy in 1974. I was not convinced of the theory behind the work until I had an experience with two of my patients at Bellevue Psychiatric Hospital.

> When I worked at Bellevue Psychiatric Hospital, two of my patients, Celia and Tommy, devised unique head devices to protect them from receiving different frequencies through their craniums. These were made from hanger wires, pieces of cans, and aluminum foil. Everyday they searched the streets for new pieces of foil and tin to maximize their protection.
>
> I spent a good amount of time trying to understand Celia and Tommy who were in their own way very intelligent people. Tommy had a college degree in mathematics and Celia had had two years of art school. They were New York "street people," acting crazy only when they needed to check into the hospital for a good meal. Other than that, they were able to fend for themselves.
>
> I asked them why they wore their special head protectors. Tommy told me that one day he began hearing voices and couldn't tune them out. He said they were both sensitive to different frequencies, and sometimes they heard voices. He told me his theory about increased radio waves and how our head functions as a

receiver for these waves. His head gear helped him block out or dull these frequencies and voices.

One day I asked Celia if I could remove a piece of foil from her head protector. She agreed, but only for a few moments. I removed a small piece of aluminum foil. Her face changed drastically, and she began to talk in fast jibberish. Tommy got upset. He understood what she was saying. I immediately put the foil back in place. Celia's face relaxed. She couldn't remember what had just happened.

That evening I kept thinking about my experience with Celia. Her speaking reminded me of my boyhood experiences listening to the Pentacostals speaking in tongues. I began to wonder if Tommy and Celia were tuned into similar voices. Maybe the voices and frequencies they perceived were real. Maybe their cranial devices really did do something. My thoughts about Tommy and Celia always seemed like forbidden territory and bordering on the insane. At that time, I didn't share them with my peers at Bellevue but kept them to myself for fear of being misunderstood.

On the other end of the "head device" spectrum are royal crowns made from precious metals and stones. Some people thought the kings and queens who wore these crowns were gifted with divine blood and were able to receive divine messages from spirits. The precious metals and stones of their crowns served as amplification devices for receiving divine guidance for their kingdoms. Whereas Tommy and Celia wore their "crowns" to block out frequencies, the kings and queens wore their crowns to receive messages.

In 1975, I met an osteopath from England who explained to me that the bones of the cranium were mobile. He told me that a branch of Osteopathic medicine known as Cranial Osteopathy was devoted only to the cranium. He said the founder, Dr. William Gurner Sutherland, invented a head device to prove his theory of cranial bone mobility. The devise was made to fit over the cranium with a system of screws, which applied pressure to cranial bones. Through experimentation on himself, he proved that restriction of cranial bone mobility could produce symptoms like headaches, body aches and pains, changes in thinking and mood, and may even be the source of certain diseases.

While I was being told the story of Dr. Sutherland and his cranial device, I couldn't help but remember my experiences with Tommy and Celia. I later learned that towards the end of his career Dr. Sutherland gave lectures on "liquid light" waves of energy passing through our cranium. I began to think Tommy and Celia were intuitively aware of something which Dr. Sutherland had been investigating from a grounded scientific perspective.

To stimulate suture mobility, tap the Otto 32 and slowly run it along any cranial suture. The photos below show the cranial sutures. One suture pass is adequate. Do not do more than two passes over a suture in a session.

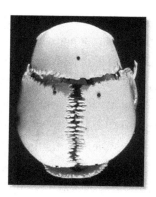 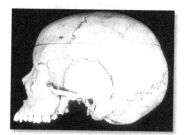

Peripheral Nerve Session

The peripheral nervous system consists of sensory receptors that are activated by a change in our internal or external environment. A stimulus to a receptor is converted to an electronic signal and transmitted to the central and/or autonomic nervous system where it can have an impact on different organs as well as how we think. The peripheral nerves are not well protected and are exposed to toxins and mechanical injuries.

Tapping the Otto 32 tuning fork and gently moving it over the skin will stimulate the peripheral nervous system and help it repair itself.

Anechoic Dream

A large animal prowled through twisted shadows without a source and unknown destination. I felt its presence only by sensations through my body as I walked through the spaces between the shadows and discovered a pond suspended above my head. I was wondering "How could water levitate?" And that is when I heard the sound of thousands of voices lifting and suspending the pond on a cushion of resonant humming.

I began to hum their sound and found myself transported into the water of the pond looking upwards into the sunlight. The water was crystal clear, and the sunbeams refracted into hundreds of different prisms filled with thousands of colors.

I gradually changed the pitch of my humming to make a different sound among myself and the others. My humming sent waves of sound outwards through the twisted shadows into the clear water of the pond bursting into thousands of colors. I hummed wave upon wave until a hole in the fabric of dreams opened within a veil of spiralling colors.

I began searching for the prowling animal by changing the pitch of my humming to resonate with the sound of the animal. It was then that I began to sense a link between the humming group and the animal as the animal's sonic image began to return and form in my awareness.

I looked upward into the pond and hummed the exact sound of the animal. The pond water became agitated and then burst into thousands of bubbles of deep sadness. Suddenly, it began to rain sensations of multicolored sounds. I thought the pond was falling, and I looked downward. Then I realized that the heads of all the humming people were tilted backward and that thousands of colored sound droplets were falling into their throats.

Planet Tuning Forks
and the Music of the Spheres

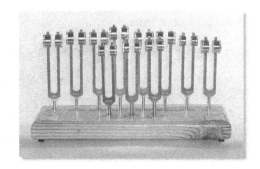

The planet tuning forks create a resonance between ourselves and the planets. Quantum physics teaches us that quantum particles are also waves that travel over a very large region of space. The idea that something is both a form confined to a small region of space and simultaneously a wave spread out over a very large region of space is counterintuitive. For this reason, we tend to identify with form and distance. For example, we are taught that a planet is a heavenly body millions of miles away. This is true from a form perspective; however, from a wave perspective, the tone of a planet is available right now through resonance. A radio or television station can be thousands of miles away, and we can tune into it without thinking about distance or needing to be "in the station." In a similar way, we can tune into a planet without having to be "on the planet."

Quantum physicists call the property of tuning into phenomena at a distance "non-locality." The term refers to the ability of a quantum entity such as an electron to influence another quantum particle instantaneously over any distance. It is suggested that the action of quantum particles that are in resonance retain a connection so that the actions of one will always influence the other. Non-locality has shattered the foundations of physics because actions do not have to have an observable cause over an observable space.

The old Greek concept of sympatheia asserts that all forms and processes in the universe are in *sympathetic* resonate relationships. The Stoic Hellenistic philosopher, Posidonius (first century B.C.), is credited with the doctrine of "cosmic sympathy" which lead to the Pythagorean concept of a "Music of the Spheres." The Pythagoreans assigned musical values to the stars and planets, and then they related those values to all aspects of living. Over the centuries, the concept was further developed by Plato, Cicero, Philon of Alexandria, and in the early Renaissance by Johannes Kepler.

Johannes Kepler lived from 1571 to 1630. He was a mathematician and mystic. He is credited with discovering that the Earth and planets travel about the sun in elliptical orbits, which he described in his three fundamental laws of planetary motion. Kepler believed that the planets made sounds as they whirled around the sun. At first he theorized that these sounds were harmonious based on his ear for Western musical harmony. After his discovery of elliptical planetary orbits, he still believed the planets made sounds; however, he came to a different conclusion about their harmonies. In his work, *The Harmonies of the World*, Kepler states:

"The heavenly motions are nothing but a continuous song for several voices to be perceived by the intellect, not by the ear—a music which, though discordant tensions, syncopations, and cadenzas as it were, progresses towards certain predesigned six-voiced cadences, and thereby set landmarks in the immeasurable flow of time."[7]

Planet tuning forks bring Kepler's vision of singing planets out of the realm of intellect and into the realm of human hearing. The sounds of the planet tuning forks are based on the theories and mathematical calculations of Swiss scientist, Hans Cousto.[8] In order to arrive at the tone of a planet, Cousto takes the reciprocal value of the duration of the astronomic or orbital period of the planet. It is simple, clear, and accurate. For example, the Earth has a rotation period of 24 hours, 56 minutes, and 4 seconds totaling 86,164 seconds. The reciprocal value is mathematical terminology for dividing by 1. The result of 1/86,164 is the frequency of 0.00001160577.

This frequency is inaudible; however, the sound of a planet does not depend on the normal audibility of a tone. Tones exist whether we hear them or not. A melody can resound even when it is not being played, and a composer can hear music before any sound has been made. Audibility and inaudibility are part of a continuous scale of sound. The human hearing range is limited to 16 cps to 20,000 cps. Bats, for example, are able to hear in the supersonic range of 20,000 cps to 100,000 cps. Whales and dolphins are able to perceive acoustic as well as electromagnetic waves. Bats are able to hear in the supersonic range, 20,000 cps to 100,000 cps above the highest frequencies audible to human beings.

---

[7] Johannes Kepler. *The Harmony of the World*. Trans. E. J. Aiton. American Philosophical Society, 1997.
[8] Hans Courto. *The Cosmic Octave*. Mendoncino, CA: Life Rhythm Publication, 1988.

The "law of the octave" is used to bring the sound of a planet into the audible range of a tuning fork. An octave is a doubling or a halving of a tone. Doubling or halving inaudible sounds in order to hear them is common in modern research. Recently, scientists have used the octave to transpose the sound of deep sea fish and bats from the ultrasonic range into the range of human hearing. It is also used to bring the sounds of pulsars and stars into the audible range for better understanding. When the frequency of the Earth is raised 24 octaves, which means it is doubled 24 times, it becomes the audible frequency of 191.74 cps.

Planet Tunings

Celestial Body	Rotation Time	Octaves into Audibility	Frequency in cps	Approximate Tone
Earth	365.24 days	32	136.1	
Sun	solar day	32	126.22	C#
Moon	29 days, 12 hrs	30	210.42	G#
Mercury	87.96 days	30	141.27	D
Venus	224.7 days	32	221.23	A
Mars	686.98	33	144.72	D
Jupiter	11.86 years	36	183.58	F#
Saturn	29.45 years	36	147.85	D
Neptune	164.78 years	40	211.44	A
Uranus	84.01 years	39	207.36	G#
Pluto	248.43	40	140.25	D

Each planet tone is an archetype deep in our collective unconsciousness. *The sound of each planet tuning fork activates the archetype of the planet. When we hear them, qualities are awakened within ourselves that resonate with the planet.* To describe the process, Johannes Kepler said, "...*verissimae Harmoniae archetype, qui intus est in Anima*..." — "the archetype of the truest harmony which lies within our soul."[9]

The planets have been sounding in cosmic space for millions of years. We are immersed in their vibrations, and our genes as well as those of all living beings

---

[9] Johannes Kepler. *The Harmony of the World*. Trans. E. J. Aiton. American Philosophical Society, 1997.

are tuned into the movement of the planets. Our unconscious mind knows them just as it knows how to breathe. When we are tuned into a planet or planets, their sounds unconsciously affect our behaviors. Understanding these effects and how to make them conscious in order to better integrate them is the basis of the ancient art of astrology.

Chaldean astronomers are said to have been keeping records on the movements of stars and planets for 490,000 years! Berosus, a Chaldean astronomer responsible for the birth of Greek astrology, settled on the island of Cos and taught there until he was a hundred and sixteen years old. The late first century B.C. Roman writer, Vitruvius, wrote of Berosus and the Chaldeans, "It must be allowed that we can know what affects the twelve signs, and the sun, moon and five planets, have on the course of human life, from astrology and the calculations of the Chaldeans."[10]

The Chaldeans did not separate themselves from the heavenly bodies in their observations. They felt the planets through *sympatheia*. This later lead to the hermetic axiom "as above, so below" which encapsulates the correspondence between the macrocosm and microcosm. Charles Muses believes, the "Crown Jewel of Alexandria was the doctrine of the *ordered interrelatedness of all things*, by the power of what was then termed *sympatheia*. ...To render this far-reaching thought into our analytic, scientific terms requires the sophisticated concept of holistic systems governed principally by the affinities (or antipathies) generated by resonances (or anti-resonances) in waves of some sort, i.e., in time space periodicities."[11]

The world view at the peak of Chaldean civilization was a lot different than ours. To say they were primitive or superstitious is a great misunderstanding. Instead of expressing themselves in the calculus of numbers, they chose the language of myth and symbols. What is left of their discoveries has been passed on to us through the archetypical symbols of astrology. The direct experience of being with and feeling the planets, the source of so much knowledge, can be reawakened through the planet tuning forks.

The concept of planet tuning forks and planetary resonance is not so extraordinary in the light of the discovery of a geomagnetic wave frequency known as the *Schumann Resonance*. This resonance is a magnetic pulsation between the surface

---

[10] Marcus Vitruvius Pollio. *The Ten Books on Architecture*. Trans. M.H. Morgan. New York: Dover Publications, Inc., 1960.

[11] Ibid., pg. 147.

of the earth and the ionosphere which oscillates at a frequency of 7.8 cycles per second. The same frequency has been correlated with alpha brain wave patterns and is associated with states of deep meditation. It may be the frequency of Gaia which is achieved in altered states of consciousness during shamanistic rituals. By tuning into this frequency we become one with the Earth.

Listening to any planet tuning fork or placing it on your body is like being on that planet. With the planetary tuning forks, we enter into a resonant field of the planet and are able to tune into its qualities. The following chart gives the basic qualities of each planet. It should be used in conjunction with the Tuning into the Planets exercise.

PLANET QUALITIES

Earth . . . . stability and grounding
Sun . . . . light, warmth, joy, and illumination
Moon . . . . love, sensitivity, creativity, femininity, anima
Mercury . . . . intellectuality, mobility, quickness
Venus . . . . beauty, love, sexuality, harmony
Mars . . . . force, energy, freedom, humor
Jupiter . . . . growth, success, justice, spirituality
Saturn . . . . focus, boundaries
Neptune . . . . imagination, spiritual love, secrets
Uranus . . . . spontaneity, independence, originality
Pluto . . . . power, change, crisis

Tuning into the Planets Exercises

Choose the planet you want to tune into. Sit quietly in a safe place and call in the planet. "Calling in" means that you ask for the planet to resonate with you and is a way of tuning into the wave qualities of the planet. The moment your mind acknowledges the planet through calling it in, it is like turning the dial of a radio tuner to a specific station. At this point, whether you are aware of it or not, you are receiving the planet.

Take the tuning fork that resonates with the planet and sound it. Bring it to your left ear and hum with the sound. Tap it again. Bring it to your right ear and hum with the sound. Put down the tuning fork close your eyes and hum the sound of the planet. If you are not sure that you are "in tune," then tap the tuning fork and bring it to your ears again. Allow your humming to become softer until the sound is internalized as a "thought of sound" that resonates through you.

Journal

Is there a specific communication you are receiving from the planet?

Become aware of your thoughts within the resonance of the planet.

Become aware of your emotions within the resonance of the planet.

Become aware of any changes in your body within the resonance of the planet.

Additional Observations

Brain Tuning

The Brain Tuners are tuning forks designed to use sound to signal the brain to shift into different states of awareness, called Delta, Theta, Alpha, and Beta. Each state of awareness is based on brain wave frequencies measured by electroencephalography (EEG) technology. Research shows that during a 24-hour period, we naturally shift into and out of these states of awareness in order to perform different life activities and tasks at our

maximum capability. Delta, Theta, Alpha, and Beta brain frequencies are always present on an EEG, and it is the higher amplitude frequency that determines your state of awareness. For example, if your Alpha frequency is appearing at a high amplitude, then you are in an Alpha state of awareness. Theta, Delta, and Beta brain wave cycles are also present but at lower amplitudes.

Delta

The Delta frequency is 1 cps to 3 cps and looks like this on the EEG machine.

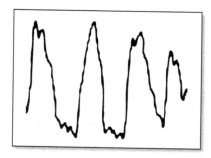

The Delta frequency is associated with deep sleep. The great yogi, Pantanjali said that quality deep sleep is a wave of thought about nothingness. During the Delta frequency, we reconnect with our source, the Universal Energy Field, which provides the energy to repair and revitalize our body and mind.

Theta

The Theta frequency is 4 cps to 6 cps and looks like this on the EEG machine.

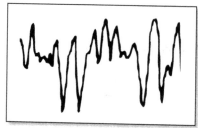

Theta is known as the twilight state and often associated with mystical experiences. It is the state we are in before we enter into deep sleep. We also find it as we rise out of deep sleep and go into waking consciousness. Theta awareness is associated with a waking dream state that is filled with vivid imagery and clear auditory perceptions. In Theta awareness, we are receptive to information from our superconscious mind and are better able to hear the voice of the healer within.

Theta is also associated with the gateway to learning and memory. While in Theta awareness, we have better access to our unconscious resources and can access more memories. It is the gateway to learning because the material we are studying can be imprinted in our unconscious mind and then accessed through Theta awareness. Often, when we know or have a strong intuition about something, we have shifted into Theta awareness and accessed important memories or learnings necessary for that moment.

Alpha

The Alpha frequency is 7 cps to 12 cps and looks like this on the EEG machine.

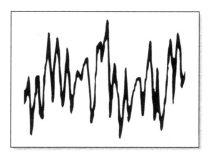

Alpha awareness is associated with being relaxed and centered during activity. In sports, Alpha awareness is called "The Zone," a state in which an athlete performs at his maximum capacity. Alpha awareness allows us to process information at a high rate, and for this reason it is associated with heightened learning. The athlete can see the entire field of play, understand what is required, and "know" exactly what to do. The average person enters Alpha awareness during problem solving which requires him to slow down and find creative solutions.

For this reason, Alpha awareness is associated with thinking outside the box. As in Theta, it has a dream-like quality; however, the Alpha dream is associated with the waking state and the requirements of daily life. When in Alpha, we can visualize our day and plan our actions. We can be introspective, creative, and see solutions that are not available in other states. Many artists and scientists talk about discovering answers or solutions to problems just before they go to sleep. Their waking mind is still working, and their awareness is expanding beyond their normal focus. Suddenly, they "see" something different and the solution appears.

Beta

The Beta frequency is 13 cps to 20 cps and looks like this on the EEG machine.

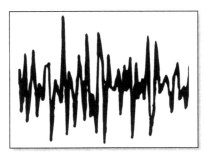

Beta awareness is associated with heightened alertness and peak concentration. While in Beta, we focus and "get things done." Our mind is moving fast, and our body follows. We see a task and immediately go for it. Our energy level is high, and we are motivated. Because our awareness is heightened, we know we can accomplish it. The mantra for Beta awareness is "go, go, go" and "do, do, do."

However, when Beta awareness dominates, it is associated with stress disorders including Type A personality, leading to burnout. Beta awareness is necessary to accomplish a task; however, it must be balanced with Alpha, Theta, and Delta. Getting things done requires the vision of Alpha, the deep resources of Theta, and the good night's sleep of Delta.

When the Brain Tuner tuning forks are simultaneously sounded, one in the left ear and the other in the right ear, the right and left hemispheres of the brain coordinate to integrate the two sounds through the difference tone between them. This difference tone is called a *binaural beat*. It is heard as a pulse moving between the two tuning forks. It is the binaural beat that synchronizes the brain with the desired state of awareness. For example, the Theta frequency is produced by sounding the fundamental Brain Tuner tuning fork, which is 256 cps in one ear, and the Delta tuning fork, which is 261 cps in the other ear. The difference tone between them, 261 cps–256 cps, is a binaural beat of 5 cps. This is a midrange Theta frequency.

Researchers believe the sensation of the binaural beat originates in the superior olivary nucleus which is located in the brain stem. This is an area of the brain that helps us locate the source of sounds in three dimensions. When you hear the binaural beat of the tuning forks, the superior olivary nucleus seeks to integrate the sounds through a mechanism that researchers call frequency following response. *The result is that the pulse of the whole brain moves towards the binaural beat of the tuning forks. This process is also called entrainment.*

Functioning at a high level of wellness requires shifting into and out of Delta, Theta, Alpha, and Beta states throughout a 24-hour period. You can visualize a car shifting in and out of different gears to meet the requirements of the road. Each gear has a different purpose, such as fast pick up, cruising, climbing hills, and slowing down. In a similar way, we need to shift in and out of different states of awareness in order to meet the challenges of life.

Shifting Awareness

The process of shifting between Delta, Theta, Alpha, and Beta begins by identifying the behaviors of your current state of awareness. To identify these behaviors, observe and note your actions and then associate them with the behaviors related to the different states of awareness. For example, you may be doing a project and simultaneously planning your next day's activities which would indicate a Beta state.

Next, tune into the felt sense of your current state of awareness. During this process, it is important to associate behaviors with your felt sense for several reasons. First, felt sense is not intellectual. After some time working with it, you will be able to identify your state of awareness without having to think about your behaviors. Second, felt sense is the gateway to perceiving the pulse of your state of awareness. The sounds of the tuning forks interact to create a binaural beat which resonates with the pulse of Delta, Theta, Alpha, and Beta. Over time, you can learn the binaural beat of the tuning forks and shift states of awareness without needing the tuning forks.

Your felt sense is a global feeling that emerges from your body. To tune into your felt sense, take a deep breath and get a sense of your whole body. At first it may appear as a body quality you may feel, like heavy, sticky, jumpy, light, fluttery, loose, or tight. When someone says, "I feel uptight" or "I feel as light as a feather," they are tuning into their felt sense and allowing descriptive words to come. Felt sense is awareness of our body consciousness, rather than our intellect.

The next step involves tuning into the rhythm of your felt sense. For example, you may have a felt sense of tightness. To amplify your felt sense, make a fist and tighten it until the tension matches with your felt sense. Next, tune into the rhythm of the tension which may appear as a slight shaking or a movement quality that underlies the tension. This will lead to a whole body sense of the rhythm of your state of awareness. In general, the rhythms range from slow to fast, with Delta being a slow rhythm and Beta being a fast rhythm.

When you have identified the behavior and tuned into the felt sense and rhythm of your current state, then select the tuning forks that resonate with that state. For example, if you have identified that you are in Alpha state, then select the Fundamental Brain Tuner tuning fork and the Alpha Brain Tuner tuning fork. Knee tap them and bring them to your right and left ears. Allow yourself to merge with the binaural beat created by the tuning forks and simultaneously associate the beat with all the qualities of your current state of awareness.

Next, ask yourself if your current state of awareness is appropriate for you in your life at the moment. If the answer is yes, then the process is finished. If the answer is no, then you need to shift into a different state of awareness. Begin by identifying the state of awareness you want. It is best to focus on a state of awareness that is either one up or one down from where you are at. For example, if you are in Beta, it is best to focus on Alpha. If you are in Alpha, you can focus on either Beta or Theta.

Choose the Brain Tuner tuning fork that is associated with the state of awareness that you want. For example, if you want to shift from Alpha to Theta, then
choose the Fundamental Brain Tuner tuning fork and the Theta Brain Tuner tuning fork. Visualize the state you want to shift into and simultaneously recall the
felt sense and rhythm of that state. Tap the Fundamental and Theta tuning forks
on your knees and bring them to your right and left ears. Allow yourself to merge
with the binaural beat created by the tuning forks.

Brain Tuner Exercise

The goal of using the Brain Tuners is to train your nervous system to recognize and shift into different states of awareness. The more your auditory
and nervous system becomes familiar with the binaural beat associated
with each state of awareness, the easier it is to shift from one state to another. The
purpose of this exercise is to train your mind and nervous system to recognize and
shift into different states of awareness.

1. Find a safe and quite place and lay out your Brain Tuner tuning forks.

2. Begin the exercise with Beta. Hold the Fundamental tuning fork in your left
    hand and the Beta tuning fork in your right hand. Visualize a felt sense of Beta
    awareness and say to yourself, "I am prepared and ready to shift into and learn
    about Beta."

3. Take a deep breath, knee tap the Brain Tuner tuning forks and bring them to
    your ears. Meditate on the Beta binaural beat and allow your body to merge
    with the sound.

4. Set the tuning forks down and close your eyes. Recall the Beta binaural beat
    and find a place in your body, called an anchor, that the felt sense of Beta can
    be located. Touch this place and say the word "Beta."

5. Take a moment and open your eyes. Go back to step two and repeat the process
    using Alpha, Theta, and Delta.

6. From Delta, work back up to the state of awareness you need to continue your
    day. For example, if you did the Brain Tuner exercise before going to bed, you
    may want to end on Theta. If you did the Brain Tuner exercise in the afternoon,
    you may want to end with Alpha or Beta.

PART 3

—————————————■—————————————

Sound Musings

Bringing Back the Muses

The study and practice of the arts develops within us an ability to appreciate the subtleties of sound, color, movement, touch, taste, and rhythm. Artistry makes life worth living. The spatial and visual arrangement of foods is as important as taste for the Japanese. The flow and movement of the Chinese martial art Tai Chi Chuan is far more important than learning how to defeat an opponent. A massage with a sense of flow and rhythm becomes a special "work of art." Without these qualities, massage is a mechanical preprogrammed event. A doctor with a sense of timing and resonance in his voice brings a healing "bedside manner."

A sense of personal artistry creates a necessary foundation for a scientist to do his work. Albert Einstein discovered the theory of relativity while playing his violin. Playing music led him into creative understandings of the universe which he then translated into numbers. He carried his violin with him wherever he went. Scientists without a sense of artistry are technicians who know what will happen if they press a button. How they press the button, the process of being present to press the button, and their relationship to their environment while they press the button are unimportant.

The nourishment of artistic qualities in athletics is important. Amy Alcott of the Ladies Professional Golf Association refers to herself as an artist when she plays golf. She talks about her training in music and painting as a necessary preparation for appreciating the subtleties of choices to be made during a round of golf. For her playing golf is like painting a picture.

The muses are everywhere and always with us. At any moment they may whisper in our ears.

Energy is
heard as sound
felt as movement
seen as color
tasted as flavor
smelled as odor
Listen.......

PRELUDE

The energy pulls, turns, and tugs us through currents and channels. Images appear and disappear, feelings rise and fall like breezes and great winds. We are loose on an inner ocean; there is no turning back. We must navigate with our inner ears, listen beyond ourself, then turn and adjust our direction. We listen for the homing frequency. The frequency draws us on.

We are like dolphins swimming into a submerged Atlantis. We are singing in rising underwater pitches, sounding to find our way. When our pitches are right we resonate and suddenly vibrate like tuning forks. We become the homing frequency. There can be no mistake. We are home.

Resonance

"It don't mean a thing if you ain't got that swing." — Duke Ellington

Resonance comes from the Latin verb *resonare,* meaning to "return to sound." It means to sound and resound as in an echo. Usually we think of resonance in terms of objects such as bells which when struck continue to ring or resonate the original sound. Another type of resonance is called sympathetic resonance. When we strike a tuning fork, another tuning fork of the same pitch will begin to vibrate with the first fork. Resonance can be understood as a merging created when energy moves back and forth between two or more bodies.

The opposite of resonance is dissonance. Dissonance happens when energy moves back and forth between two or more bodies without merging into unified pulsation. The pulses beat against one another. Resolution happens when dissonance becomes resonance. Our personal sensations of dissonance, resolution, and resonance in our daily lives serve as sonic guides. Learning to listen to, differentiate, and appreciate these sensations in daily life is fundamental to quality living.

When we meet somebody special or do something just right, we experience resonance. The longer lasting and deeper the experience of resonance, the more ecstatic we become. Our language is filled with words that ring with the taste of resonance. "Being in tune" or "we are on the same wave length" describe resonant experiences. Making the connection, being in the groove, or just plain "wow!" are further examples. When something is just right, we say "it clicks."

Imagine that the whole universe—everything we know, including cars, computers, airplanes, houses, buildings, lakes, oceans, continents, our bones, flesh, and nerves is a fountain of dream images generated and sustained by a submerged sound. Further, imagine that everything we do and think, whether good or bad, moral or immoral, is an attempt to seek out and merge with that sound. Our goal is to return to the source of the fountain. Although we may identify with the object of value, i.e., a man or woman, a car, etc., the real attraction is the resonance we experience when in the presence of that person or thing. The experience vibrates us like a tuning fork and becomes a sonic homing buoy confirming our inner journey.

As children, our playfulness leads us from one resonant experience to another. Teeter-totters, swings, kites grabbing the wind at the right moment, catching or hitting a baseball, riding a bike, skipping a rock, and bonding with a doll or stuffed animal are all part of the magic of a child's world. Children soon learn the value of pushing forward or leaning backward on a swing. They will try again and again until they get the "right feeling" of the swing. This is a moment when the thrust of the pump harmonizes exactly with the natural rhythm of the swing. They don't need classes or intellectual reasons. Their sense of resonance, which they somehow "just know," becomes both their guide and goal.

Pretend that you are an ethereal being floating in drifting currents of light. One day you begin to hear special sounds. There are two sounds, and they are beginning to merge. Your light body begins to pulsate. Surrendering to the sounds, you enter an ecstatic state of resonance.

When we arrive in our new bodies, we immediately seek resonance. A baby bonds with its mother and father. Watching a newborn baby and mother together is a wonderful experience. Their bodies are like tuning forks that vibrate in unison. I remember the indescribable feeling of the birth of my son. I am in the delivery room surrendering to the rhythm of labor. Push after push, I breath in unison with my wife as my son pulsates his way into the world.

In the new quantum physics, matter is perceived as resonant particles. Particles are created when electrons and protons are accelerated to near the speed of light. Collisions create a burst of energy in which a particle takes form. The energy of the collision keeps resonating or feeding back into itself like a bell that is struck and continues to ring.

In the universe of particle physics, matter is simultaneously a particle and a wave. Because it is a wave, each particle is also a specific frequency or vibration. Therefore, in the subatomic world, the way something vibrates determines what it is. Remember that not every collision creates a particle; only the collisions that resonate create particles. Physicists who explore the subatomic world for particles call what they are doing "resonance hunting."

The physicist, Werner Heisenberg, borrowed two words from Aristotle—*potentia* and *actuality*—to describe his experience of the quantum reality. The world "not looked at" was potential. For Heisenberg, the quantum wave was a picture of the unexamined potential of reality. Quantum waves are not existence or actuality, but the tendencies towards existence. The parallels between "musical experience" and the subatomic reality are remarkably similar. Physicists seem to rely mostly on numbers and instrumentation to "see" and map resonances. An artist relies on his or her senses and intuitions.

Communication is a resonance between two or more people. Cognitive resonance occurs when someone talks about an idea or concept that we agree with. Politicians always speak in generalities to heighten their chances for cognitive resonance with potential voters. Emotionally, we speak of affective resonance. It is the source of the terms sympathy, antipathy, empathy, telepathy, and apathy. When we pick up emotional states and feelings from another person, we say we are sympathetic. The person with the feelings is like a tuning fork setting off similar feelings in another person. If the other person is opposed to the feelings, then he resists and becomes dissonant or without resonance. This is antipathy. Empathy is a state of merging with another person's feelings. We allow ourselves to resonate with the vibratory field of the other until we are the other.

The ideal is to remain conscious of our self during the empathetic response. Conscious empathy is the foundation of healing arts and the key for understanding another person's experience. When we are empathic, distance as we know it ceases to exist. We are both in the same resonating field. It is therefore possible to experience the other at great distances. This is the telepathic response or feeling response at a distance. Apathy means no feeling. When one is apathetic, there is no resonance.

Resonate communication on a spiritual level is called communion. Although health professionals are trained to focus their attention on mental, emotional, or physical processes during empathic response with their clients, they often report a special communion between themselves and their patients.

Faith healers bypass these levels and focus only on the spiritual. They lay their hands on the body and allow themselves to empathetically resonate wherever spirit leads them. The resulting interaction between the person and healer becomes a divine communion. A resonate "returning to sound" creates a healing response. In this sense, regardless of academic training or analytical understanding, we all must become faith healers for our insights and studies to be effective.

I remember a story told by Elisabeth Kübler-Ross. She was in charge of training psychiatrists to counsel dying people. The young doctors knew a lot about the psychodynamics of dying as well as the physical condition of the patients. However, Kübler-Ross noticed that when the medical doctors left the room after speaking with the patient, the patient was quite often agitated and upset.

One day she noticed that when the cleaning lady left the patients' rooms, they were at peace with themselves, breathing easier, and more open to talking. She asked the cleaning lady what she was doing. The cleaning lady, who hadn't even graduated from grade school, said she had experienced a lot of death in her family. She said she just "felt" for the people and would just sit with them a moment while she cleaned up. Kübler-Ross realized that her ability to "just sit" and be with a dying person was what the doctors lacked. To the dismay of her colleagues, she made the cleaning lady her assistant instructor.

The experience of empathetic resonance through touching has been given many names by bodyworkers. Dr. John Upledger calls it "melding" and sees it as the prerequisite of all good bodywork. "The idea is to meld the palpating part of your body with the body you are examining. As this melding occurs, the palpating part of your body does what the patient's body is doing. It becomes synchronized… The objective is to have that part of your body, which is examining and palpating a patient, do exactly what the patient's body is doing and would otherwise be doing even if you weren't there." Dr. Milton Tragger, the founder of Tragger Therapy, uses the term "hook-up" to describe empathetic resonance. Dr. Randolph Stone, the founder of Polarity Therapy, called empathetic resonance "tuning into the energy."

The synchronization of bodies is traditionally called "achieving rapport" in verbal counseling. In Neuro-Linguistic Programming, it is called "pacing." Without pacing, there can be no communication. The research of Dr. William Condon uses microanalysis of filmed human interaction to reveal precise synchronization of rhythmic body movements between two people interacting. This synchrony is invisible to the eye and unconscious to the participants.

Dr. Milton Erickson considered it a necessity to "get into a patient's reality." He would sometimes spend years understanding and piecing together a patient's view of the world, body movements, and speech patterns. The psychiatrist, R. D. Laing, illustrates the principle of "getting into a patient's reality" in his description of a "Schizophrenic Voyage." Laing would spend days with a patient to the point of even being in a closet with them to experience resonance with their reality.

The resonant experience of love is so powerful that we sometimes would do anything not to lose it. First there is resonance.

In her eyes I perceive myself as mysterious, unknown, exciting, and vibrant. She is the lover that awakens my heart, and each throb is a revelation, a vision, and a dream that becomes a remembrance of who I am. She is the embodiment of the sweetest elixir. We drink and meld until the other disappears into the mists and is devoured by the force of union.

The experience is so magnificent that we want it to happen forever. However, the moment we try to keep the experience, the feeling is gone. The same person that we fell in love with is suddenly different. It is as though we reached out and put the palm of our hand on a ringing bell in an effort to keep it ringing forever. We are shocked when the quality of the ringing diminishes. To make things worse, we grab the bell even tighter and sometimes even hit it to get it to ring again. Eventually we give up. We cannot sustain this "grabbing energy." We say the "life is out of the relationship" or "the thrill is gone."

During a session, a client described his relationship with his wife as "the ring is gone." He had done everything to get it back. And it became clear from the tone of his voice that "everything" meant every possible way of grabbing and holding onto her. Resonance, or the ringing bell quality of a relationship is only nourished through surrender. This implies giving up the other in order to have the other. It seems like a paradox. Experienced from sonic consciousness, it becomes very real.

Everyone wants resonance. Regardless of our behaviors, relationships, occupations, looks, cultures, lifestyles, and tastes, we are listening for resonance. With each experience of resonance we move closer to our source. The closer we come to our source, the more we are "beings of sound mind and body." Resonance is everywhere and always available to us. Everyone has a front row seat in the cosmic concert.

INTERLUDE

Trash on the street in the form of papers and dried leaves

is picked up by a gust of wind and swirled upwards in spi-

rals and loops creating twisting, meandering patterns. Each

piece of differently-shaped paper, discarded and unimport-

ant, suddenly becomes living, pulsating, and mobile through

an invisible merger with floating, dipping, gliding, bending,

and twisting air. Listen...the spiritual master is everywhere.

Dissonance

Learning to identify, understand, and honor dissonance leads to new levels of living and wellness. Dissonance means without sonic alignment or to "beat against." Our first reactions to dissonances, whether in music or life, are to label them undesirable and something to be avoided. When Igor Stravinsky premiered *The Rite of Spring,* many listeners rioted. They cited the horrible dissonances in the music as the cause. A group of doctors tried to sue Stravinsky for damaging peoples ears. Today many find the dissonances in *The Rite of Spring* to be harmonious.

During the Middle Ages, the Catholic Church determined what musical tones and intervals were spiritual. New musical sounds were usually introduced through heresy and thought to be the work of the devil. As hard as it is to believe, many people were executed and tortured for playing the "wrong note."

Go to the piano key board and play C and G then play the octave of C and G. If you lived in the Dark Ages, you might have been on your way to being a music star. Now play C and C followed by C and F#. Uh-oh! You made a fatal mistake. You are now on your way to being burned at the stake or worse. C and F# were considered to be the interval of the devil.

Our life experiences of dissonance vary greatly. A commonly used word for dissonance is stress. Dr. Hans Selye defines stress as adaptation to change. Those that resist change will perceive stress as distress. Those that accept change may experience the same stress as euphoria or U-stress. In other words, what is distress for one person may be euphoria for another. This may explain from a scientific perspective why the dissonances of a music composition like Stravinsky's Rite of Spring may be terrible for one person and beautiful for another.

The process of a child learning to swing illustrates the principle of dissonance as a necessary component of acquiring a new skill. The child learns to pull on the swing at just the right time through hundreds of misses. Because missed pulls are out of alignment with the desired feeling of swinging, they are perceived by the child as frustrating. "How can I learn to swing if I keep pulling and nothing happens!"

Eventually, by watching other children, getting hands-on help from parents, and achieving many mini successes, the child begins to internalize a "right feeling" of swinging. The misses contrasted to the "right feeling" may ironically lead to increasing states of dissonance. When we have no idea of the right way, the wrong way is acceptable. When we experience the right way, the wrong way seems even more dissonant.

One day something happens, a right movement, an "accident," or somebody says something that "makes sense," and suddenly the child knows how to swing. He can pull on the swing again and again at just the right moment. From this moment on, the child knows how to swing for the rest of his life.

The Nobel Prize winning physicist, Dr. Ilya Prigogine, discovered the importance of dissonance while investigating chemical systems. He termed his discoveries "order from chaos." Prigogine proved that for a system to change and go into a higher state of functioning, it must first pass through a state of disruption or chaos. The sonic term for chaos is dissonance.

Prigogine points out the crucial role dissonance plays in living systems evolving into higher levels of order. He discovered that over time all living systems dissipate more and more energy caused by fluctuations or dissonances inherent within the system. As time passes, these dissonances increase in intensity, causing the system to move further and further from equilibrium. Soon everything begins to wobble. The wobbling increases until all preexisting order within the system shatters causing the system to leap into chaos.

Prigogine terms the precise moment a system goes from order to chaos a bifurcation point. As a system approaches bifurcation, it only takes a very small and seemingly inconsequential event to create chaos. From chaos the system reorganizes itself into a new system functioning at a higher-level resonance.

Whether the resonance is a higher or lower level than the original system is determined by what mathematicians call "strange attractors." Strange attractors can be visualized as seeds of the new order sown during the old order. For example, a child learning to swing builds attractors through mini successes, modeling other children, and positive encouragement. When the old order falls apart, the new order reforms around the vibration of these experiences.

The pictures on the next page are computer generated images of chaos. They are based on the fractal mathematic equations of Benoit Mandelbrot. When looking at the pictures, visualize them as a system at the moment of bifurcation. They are the highest intensity of dissonance before a system transforms into a new state of resonance.

Meditating on these images reveals that dissonance has its own special beauty. This is another explanation of the always-changing notions of what is or is not dissonant in music as well as life. When the listener surrenders to dissonance, he or she is transformed into a new order.

We must learn to listen to and appreciate dissonance in our life. For example, an alarm clock is dissonant for our sleeping self. However, for our waking self, the alarm clock is a sound we created to remind us to wake up. Oftentimes we forget that our waking self set the alarm. The alarm annoys us. We get angry. Maybe we throw our alarm clock across the room. When we surrender to the message, we awake and remember, "Today I got up early to begin my vacation. Thank goodness for that alarm, or I would have missed my plane."

From a sound healing perspective, the experiences of dissonance are our inner alarm system. When an alarm goes off, something is going to change whether we think we are going to like it or not. The more we resist alarms, the more the intensity of dissonance increases in our life.

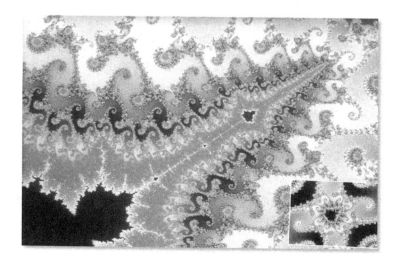

We must learn to appreciate dissonance and actively listen to our inner alarms. The following "dissonance ear training," is to help us tune into our alarms and wake up. Each volume level is like an alarm clock getting louder and louder. We are free to wake up at any volume.

DISSONANCE LEVEL 1: "Not Quite Right Feeling"

We recognize a vague feeling of discomfort or our inner voice whispers a warning. Oftentimes our body slightly tightens. Sometimes we may perceive a subtle feeling of pulling away. The intensity of the alarm is low enough to easily overlook or dismiss. It is the kind of message that we recognize in hindsight and say "I should have listened" or "I had a feeling."

DISSONANCE LEVEL 2: Minor Problem

We have progressed beyond the "not quiet right feeling" and can consciously, if only for a moment, identify the source of irritation. A friend or relative doesn't clean up after themselves in the house, and we don't say anything. It is even uncomfortable for us to do their cleaning; however, it is a small problem. The discomfort soon leaves. Oftentimes we will tell ourselves a story: "It is OK. He will be leaving in a few days. He is such a good person, it is worth it to do these things for him just to have him here." Although we may even come to believe our stories, which in psychological terms is the beginning of denial, our bodies always tighten when faced with a minor problem.

DISSONANCE LEVEL 3: Major Problem

The source of irritation is clear and in our consciousness for long periods of time. It is increasingly difficult to tell ourselves stories. We know something is wrong and that there is a problem. The person went from occasionally throwing something on the floor, leaving papers, tracking in dirt, to overstaying his welcome and playing the stereo late at night. Even our neighbors are complaining.

However, it is still possible to somehow put off our problem. We tell ourselves more stories: "If I am nicer, maybe he will go away. It's not his fault. He had a hard childhood. Maybe his behavior has something to do with me." At this level of dissonance, everyone knows we have a problem except us. When we finally do something about it, everyone is relieved. When we keep denying, then the problem goes to a higher level of dissonance.

DISSONANCE LEVEL 4: Crisis

The dissonance is loud and screeching. We can't get away from it. It is with us everywhere we go. Our whole universe seems to be shaking and falling apart. In psychotherapeutic language, we are "bottoming out," and there is no place left to go but up. We have to face the dissonance. Many people tell stories of reaching the bottom and finding a new life.

I learned a long time ago not to judge people at the bottom. While working at Bellevue Psychiatric Hospital, I was called as a therapist to a flophouse on the Bowery. We were trying to extend our services into the community and help people before they reached hospitalization stage. On this occasion, I walked into a small dirty room that smelled of human waste with cockroaches running from wall to wall. In the room there was a man covered with spit laying on a dirty bed and a priest sitting next to him preparing to give last rites. I was disgusted that I should be called to such a place and angry with this man for letting his life depreciate to such a low level.

For some reason I stayed. As the priest gave the last rites, the man on the bed opened his eyes and said, "I see Jesus." Suddenly, he began to glow. I actually felt the vibration in the room increase. As I looked at this dying man, he suddenly became soft and radiant. I could feel his energy enveloping the room. I felt as though I was blessed and showered with grace.

All of this lasted just a few minutes by the clock and an eternity from my inner time perspective. When he exhaled his last breath, this filthy disgusting drunk had transformed into one of the most important spiritual teachers of my life. He taught me that a crisis can be an opportunity for extraordinary growth and that I should be very humble in my judgements of other people's life dissonance.

Jacob's Ladder

The ancient story of Jacob's Ladder illustrates the mythological relationship between dissonance and order. Jacob's Ladder is an archetypical ladder between Heaven and Earth. We begin as spiritual beings at the top of the ladder and descend until we become earthly beings at the bottom of the ladder. Our spiritual journey begins when we choose to climb back up the ladder. Each rung upwards represents increasing states of energy and consciousness.

The transitions from one rung to another on Jacob's Ladder are different than a regular ladder. The rungs are in discontinuous steps. This means that the distance between each rung becomes greater and greater the further we go up the ladder.

Climbing Jacob's Ladder requires a special climbing skill which is sometimes referred to as "quantum leaping." We are at one level of vibration or rung on the ladder, then suddenly we are at another. We literally leap from one rung, something like excited electrons jumping from one orbit to another, and changing the nature of an atom.

The myth of Jacob's Ladder is very real in our everyday life. The process of moving into different states of energy begins with dissonance. During dissonance, our life becomes challenged. The more we deny our challenge, the greater our dissonance becomes. There are no solutions on our current rung of the ladder. We must seek change and seek resolutions from a higher perspective.

I have come to believe the man I worked with in the Bowery was on a very high rung of the ladder. He resisted the jump to the next rung until the last moment. During his last rights, he surrendered to whatever internal dissonance he had been avoiding. He made what appeared to be an inconceivable leap. His gift was to show me that at any moment dissonance may transform into a new and higher state of resonance.

Rhythm

know whether a movie will be good by listening to the music. Creative film composers have a natural ability to relate music with life. Movies without good sound tracks would lose most of their appeal. In recent years, movie theaters have installed special "surround sound" systems. Today we are more aware than ever of the importance of "background" music.

All good comedians talk about the importance of rhythm and timing. I love to watch Marx Brothers movies. The rhythm and timing of their actions create a special musical reality. One is drawn into their absurd world. Their stories always seem to come from their rhythm. They were all natural musicians with a great sense of rhythm. Chico, Harpo, and Zeppo would hire the Los Angeles Symphony Orchestra to play with them on Sundays. Groucho said he hated this and claimed he could care less about music.

W. C. Fields was one of the world's greatest jugglers as well as a comedian. When I watched old film strips of him juggling, I was amazed at his sense of rhythm and timing. In his movies, people seem to juggle their lives in crazy ways giving rise to funny juggled words which make sense in a juggled reality. I could sense his comedy and comic language coming from this inner rhythm.

I used to love to walk with my grandfather through the Crown Hill Cemetery in Indianapolis. We didn't talk much. He was a very quiet man from Kentucky. He had a wonderful walking rhythm. I remember the feeling of being drawn into his pace and the special quality of our walks. We would always walk in silence to the top of Crown Hill and visit a memorial that looked like an ancient Greek temple. He would always break our silence and tell me the memorial was the resting place of the famous poet James Whitcomb Riley. We would throw pennies on the floor of the memorial before walking back down the hill in silence.

I remember feeling the rhythms of cats and dogs, thunder and lightning, and the movements of night and day. I remember sensing the interactive rhythms of my parents, sisters, grandparents, aunts, and cousins. When I discovered the piano, I immediately began to play those rhythms. I couldn't care less about the notes. I would just tune into the rhythm and play musical stories about walking, thunder, cats and dogs fighting, and on and on.

After years of formal piano training, I woke up one day and realized that I was no longer playing from my inner sense of rhythm. I become lost in notes and counting. Out of desperation and panic I called Sophia Rosoff, a piano teacher recommended by a friend whose playing I respected. Sophia began our lessons by telling me there was only one rule passed on to her from her teacher, Abby Whiteside, and that was to never break the emotional rhythm of a composition.

Music must come from a place of inner rhythm. The classical pianist discovers the composer's emotional rhythm, merges with that rhythm, and the music emerges naturally. Intellectual knowledge is the last thing that students come to learn. During a great class, a teacher tunes into the rhythm of his students and allows his lecture presentation to come from those rhythms. Students learn through rhythmic synchronization, and when this happens, the teacher feels like they are conducting an orchestra.

I studied Ayurvedic medicine with Dr. Vincent Ladd. Dr. Ladd began every class by tuning into the rhythm of his students. We would sit in silence. At the right moment, Dr. Ladd would burst into song and sing the Vedas we were to study that day. The whole day would then proceed from special Vedic rhythms. Years later I sometimes forgot the particulars of lecture; however, I have never forgotten the inner rhythms of the Vedas.

When I counsel couples, I have them talk with one another while I observe. Although I listen to what they are saying, my main observation involves tuning into the way their bodies move together as they communicate. I allow myself to sense their rhythms. When their bodies move together, I know they are communicating. When they begin to go slightly out of sync, I know they are getting ready to show me what they came for. When they manifest two different rhythms with no apparent relationship between them, I know they are having a problem.

I have learned that the content or story of their problem is always secondary to their rhythm. I remember telling a story to a couple that had nothing to do with what they were talking about. During the telling of the story, I merged the feeling of their different and dissonant rhythms. As I felt an inner merger, the couple began to cry. Suddenly, they understood each other. At that moment, we were all in rhythm together. It did not matter what we said. I decided to teach them to disagree and argue in rhythm. We had a great time.

When we lose track of our inner rhythms, illness results. The old nature cures of Europe involved going to a sanitarium and returning to the rhythms of nature. The sanitariums were quiet places located in natural surroundings. While at the sanitarium, the patient was put on a rhythmic schedule and given natural foods. Every day patients would sit, enjoy their surroundings, go for walks, sunbathe, breathe fresh air, and bathe in special waters.

Contrast the nature cure sanitariums to the current day rhythm of our modern hospitals. The word that best describes the hospitals I have worked in is "discombobulated." With fluorescent lighting, stale air, processed food and water, harsh sounds including TV's, telephones, and radios blaring, and being woken up all hours by beeping, it is no wonder people are afraid of going to a hospital.

Music School

Life is a song. It has its own rhythm of harmony. It is a symphony of all things which exist in major and minor keys of Polarity. It blends the discords, by opposites into harmony which unites the whole into a grand symphony of life. To learn through experience is to blend with the whole, it is object of our being here.

— Dr. Randolph Stone, founder of Polarity Therapy

I call learning about and resolving our personal challenges music school. Everyone is enrolled. We are all working towards our masters degree. In this school, whether we like it or not, we must learn about dissonance and resonance. Fortunately, music school is a school without walls and we don't have to pay money for our lessons unless we want to. It is a funny school in that some people pay money not to have lessons, and it always seems like lots of people are trying to "play hooky."

Sometimes it looks like there are a lot of music school dropouts. Unfortunately for them, the law, sometimes called the "Word of God," says that they must finish school and pass all their tests at the 100% level. The truant officers like St. Peter and Mr. Lucifer are very strict. Fortunately for us, we have all the lifetimes we want to get through school. I have heard of people who have been studying for several million years.

Sometimes our personalities do not understand they are in music school. Our personalities like to make up stories, rearrange things, and spend a lot of time looking good for other personalities. They can't understand when things sometimes go wrong.

We need to understand our problems are just dissonances seeking resonance. We have a special opportunity to learn about a new level of energy and make a quantum leap in awareness. Unfortunately, when we are having problems they are considered a judgment of ourselves. Sometimes we go to a professional therapist, and this really means are in trouble and our neighbors better not find out!

We need to be told that experiencing dissonance is a natural state. Dissonance is beautiful. During dissonance we are like a caterpillar becoming a butterfly. We are getting ready to transform into a new form. Instead, we are often told that there is something wrong with our personalities. It's not surprising that everybody tries to hide their dissonance and act consonant. I call it the "Who! Me have dissonance!" or the "Alfred E. Newman Syndrome."

We sooner or later learn that it is impossible to hide dissonance. Hidden dissonance sneaks out and attracts more dissonance. Some personalities even come to understand the old saying that what you resist will persist.

When we try to hide our dissonance, it doesn't take long before more dissonant friends show up. They want to have dissonance fun. When a nice person withholding anger meets another nice person withholding anger, they have a good time blaming each other in a nice way. Sometimes they even forget they are nice people and blow up. Then they say, "That wasn't me."

When dissonance is pushed into your body, it causes different organs to vibrate in dysfunctional ways. Eventually you get a physical disease. Then you say "How did I catch that?"

Then one day, usually in the middle of a crisis, we hear...

"My dearest one, you are a being of Sound composed of many tones. Your body's shape, movements, desires, motivations, and wellness are determined by your inner concert. The source of your concert is a core of Sound beyond your wants and desires. Listen and the Sound will heal you.

This is Music School. Everything you know and feel is Sound. Learn to dance with your dissonances. Your partners may look strange. You may feel them as anger, grief, sadness, fear, and despair. However, once you listen, they will transform into beautiful sounds.

The spiritual concert is everywhere. When you dance, your body organs will make sounds, and your muscles will play the correct tones. Your voice will sing praises, and the stars will shine upon you.

Use your ears... Graduation day is near."

Endings

GLOSSARY OF TERMS

———■———

cps The letters cps stand for *cycles per second*. Tuning forks are precise instruments and, therefore, we need to know exactly how many times they vibrate
in one second. For example, if your tuning fork says 128 cps, then this means
that the prongs move back and forth 128 times in one second. The higher the
cps, the higher the pitch of the sound; conversely, the lower the number, the
lower the pitch of the sound.

Fundamental Tone The fundamental tone is the first and lowest note of the harmonic or overtone series. Everything begins with the fundamental.

Harmonics The term *harmonics* is another word for overtones. Some people say,
"Did you hear those harmonics?" while others will say, "Did you hear the
overtones." They are both talking about the same sounds.

Hertz Scientists also use the term hertz, abbreviated Hz, to describe cycles per
second. For example, 1Hz is equal to 1 cps. The term hertz is named after the
German scientist, Heinrich Hertz, for his work with electromagnetic waves.

Interval The space or difference between two tones is called an *interval*. For
example, the difference between a C256 cps tuning fork and a G384 cps is
called the interval of a fifth. An interval is also a ratio.

Note *Notes* are given letters. For example, we call a note C, D, E, F, G, A, or B.
Notes are musical tones. The exact pitch of a note is determined by the cps
of that note and its interval relationship with other notes. It is important to
understand that there are many different C's. Just because we say that a note
is C does not tell us the exact cps of the note. If we want to be precise, we must
know the cps.

Octave We call the relationship an *octave* because it contains 8 (octa) tones. The
top tone of the octave is an exact double of the lower tone. Every possible

interval relationship is contained in the space of an octave. For this reason, the Greeks called the octave diapason, which meant "through all possibilities." Similarly, alchemists, mystics, and spiritual philosophers oftentimes refer to the "octaves" of creation or the different octaves of creation. These are always relative divisions based on the author's understanding of creation.

Otto Tuning Fork   An *Otto tuning fork* is a normal tuning fork with weights added to the prongs. The weights cause the tuning fork to transmit more vibration through the stem. For this reason, these tuning forks are excellent for placing directly on the body.

Overtones   The word *overtone* means sounds over sounds. Imagine a fountain fed by one stream of water. As the water leaves the pipe it divides into many streams of water. Now imagine one sound becoming many sounds. These sounds, like a fountain, are called overtones. When we tap two tuning forks together, we create overtones.

Pitch   *Pitch* is a relative term that refers to high and low sound quality of a tuning fork. For example, if the tone of your tuning fork is high, it has a high pitch. If it is low, it has a low pitch.

Protocol   A *protocol* is a specific sequence of sounds used for learning about tuning forks as well as for healing.

Ratio   A *ratio* is the mathematical relationship of two tones. For example, the interval of a fifth is 256 cps / 384 cps. If we divide the numbers to their common denominator, the ratio is 2/3. A ratio is also an interval.

Sine Wave   A *sine wave* is a pure wave of sound without overtones. Gently tapping a tuning fork on the knee will sound a sine wave.

Tone   A *tone* is a wave of sound that has definite cycles per second. A wave of sound is defined in cycles per second where one wave is one cycle. The number of cycles in a second, abbreviated cps, defines the exact tone of a sound. The less the cps, the lower the tone. The greater the cps, the higher the tone. Tone accuracy was first measured in cycles per second in 1834 when a group of German physicists using a mechanical stroboscopic tested a tuning fork.

Tuning Fork   A *tuning fork* is a musical instrument invented in 1711 by John Shore. It consists of a stem and two prongs. When sounded, the prongs vibrate back and forth creating a precise tone.

Chemical Abbreviations

NO Nitric Oxide

NE Norepinephrine

APPENDIX A
Sounding Journal

Date _____   Location _____

Tuning Fork / Interval _____

GENERAL OBSERVATIONS / IMPRESSIONS

SPECIFIC OBSERVATIONS

Do you experience a color inside the interval, i.e., is it green, yellow, blue, red, etc?

Do you experience a temperature inside the interval, i.e., is it cool, hot, warm, or cold?

Do you receive thoughts when listening to the interval, i.e., messages, insights, stories, visions, instructions?

Do you experience specific emotions when listening to the interval?

Do you experience geometric shapes, patterns, or mathematical forms when listening to the interval?

Do you experience a shift or change in body posture when listening to the interval?

ADDITIONAL OBSERVATIONS

APPENDIX B*

Signature: Med Sci Monit, 2003; 9(5): RA116-121
PMID: 12761468

WWW.MEDSCIMONIT.COM
Review Article

Received: 2003.03.03
Accepted: 2003.04.04
Published: 2003.05.22

Sound therapy induced relaxation: down regulating stress processes and pathologies

Elliott Salamon[1], Minsun Kim[2], John Beaulieu[3], George B. Stefano[1]

[1] Neuroscience Research Institute, State University of New York at Old Westbury, NY 11568, USA
[2] The Long Island Conservatory, 1125 Willis Avenue, Albertson, NY 11507, USA
[3] BioSonic Enterprises, Ltd, P.O. Box 487, High Falls, New York 12440 USA

Summary

The use of music as a means of inducing positive emotions and subsequent relaxation has been studied extensively by researchers. A great deal of this research has centered on the use of music as a means of reducing feelings of anxiety and stress as well as aiding in the relief of numerous pathologies. The precise mechanism responsible for these mediated effects has never been truly determined. In the current report we propose that nitric oxide (NO) is the molecule chiefly responsible for these physiological and psychological relaxing effects. Furthermore this molecules importance extends beyond the mechanistic, and is required for the development of the very process that it mediates. Nitric oxide has been determined to aid in the development of the auditory system and participate in cochlear blood flow. We show that NO is additionally responsible for the induced exhibited physiological effects. We proceed to outline the precise neurochemical pathway leading to these effects. Furthermore we explore the interrelationship between the varying emotion centers within the central nervous system and explain how the introduction of music can mediate its effects via NO coupled to these complex pathways.

key words: **music • stress • relaxation • soundtherapy • nitric oxide**

Full-text PDF: http://www.MedSciMonit.com/pub/vol_9/no_5/3514.pdf
Word count: 2171
Tables: –
Figures: 1
References: 77

Author's address: George B. Stefano, Neuroscience Research Institute, State University of New York at Old Westbury, P.O.Box 210, Old Westbury, 11568 New York, NY, USA, email: gstefano@sunynri.org

*Reprinted with permission of Medical Science Monitor

APPENDIX B *(cont'd)*

Med Sci Monit, 2003; 9(5): RA116-121

1. DEFINING STRESS

The term 'stress' as defined in the strict biological sense is an event or stimulus that alters the existing homeostasis within a given organism [1]. Some theorists now refer to the 'healthy state' as one of stability in the face of change. Multiple causes of stress add to what is called 'allostatic loading', which can be pathologic if not relieved. The state may be cognitively appraised or noncognitively perceived. The disturbed organism may either acutely or chronically experience this stimulus. Indeed, the stressor (the stimulus) may even emerge from within the organism itself, such as in interoceptive psychiatric stress. Stress is difficult to define because there are many types of stressors, or stimuli, that can bring on this homeostatic perturbation. Through an extremely complicated homeostatic process, all living organisms maintain their survival in the face of both external and internal 'stressors' [2,3].

Stress when defined as a psychological phenomenon is characterized by feelings of apprehension, nervousness and helplessness, and is commonly present in patients undergoing medical procedures. Past research demonstrates that stress induces numerous types of physiological complications. Stress has been found to cause hypertension, tachycardia and hyperventilation [4], all of which were shown to be linked with ischemia and can cause fluctuations in body temperature, urinary urgency, enlarged pupils, and loss of appetite [5]. Furthermore it has been demonstrated that stress leads to increased cortisol levels, depressing the immune system. Lastly, conditions that arouse stress may actually increase pain [6]. An overwhelming amount of research has been conducted into methods of alleviating the stress response, as well as exploring possible mechanisms by which these methods act.

2. STRESS AND ITS RELATION TO MUSIC

The use of music has consistently been found to reduce stress levels of patients in clinical settings. Mulooly et al. [6] investigated the use of music for postoperative stress and found that patients who underwent an abdominal hysterectomy reported lower stress levels after listening to music when compared to patients who were not exposed to this treatment. Studies [7] have contrasted music to verbal distraction, concluding that although the methods were comparable for the reduction of stress, music was more effective in the reduction of blood pressure. Further studies find [8] that adult patients that listened to music during dialysis were found to have significantly lower blood pressure after their treatment than before. In further studies the effectiveness of music in the reduction of stress has been measured in myocardial infarction patients [8], and in coronary care units [9]. Music has been paired with other therapeutic techniques to reduce stress as well. In a study of pediatric patients, group music therapy sessions, including singing, and instrument playing, were found to decrease observed stress in children before surgery [5]. Guided imagery and music together were found to decrease pain and stress in patients undergoing elective colorectal surgery [4].

3. HOW EMOTIONS CAUSE STRESS AND HOW MUSIC ALLEVIATES IT: CNS PROCESSES

Music and its calming effects have been demonstrated to have a large emotional component. When pleasant music is heard the brains motivation and reward pathways are reinforced with positive emotion mentally linked to the music. This emotionalized memory includes many 'somatic markers', i.e, bodily sensations that accompany emotion and set the feeling tone', feels right' to the person [10]. Clearly, music and the emotion it imparts can be viewed as a process of reinforcing a positive belief so that rational thought can not hinder the strength of the belief (see [11,12]). Indeed, belief in regard to a therapy and/or doctor and/or personal religion, may in fact stimulate physiological processes, enhancing naturally occurring health processes by augmenting their level of performance. Conversely, emotional stresses such as fear and anxiety can induce cardiovascular alterations, such as cardiac arrhythmias [13–15]. These cardiovascular events can be initiated at the level of the cerebral cortex and may involve insular as well as cingulated, amygdalar and hypothalamic processes. Clinically we may see this as elevated cortisol levels and in some instances can induce sudden death in patients with significant coronary artery disease [16]. In addition, heart rate is often altered under stressful conditions. Neurons in the insular cortex, the central nucleus of the amygdala, and the lateral hypothalamus, owing to their role in the integration of emotional and ambient sensory input, may be involved in the emotional link to the cardiovascular phenomenon. These include changes in cardiac autonomic tone with a shift from the cardioprotective effects of parasympathetic predominance to massive cardiac sympathetic activation [13]. This autonomic component, carried out with parasympathetic and sympathetic preganglionic cells via subcortical nuclei from which descending central autonomic pathways arise, may therefore be a major pathway in how belief may affect cardiovascular function. The importance of music and the elicited emotional response (and therefore limbic activation) was further demonstrated in ischemic heart disease when patients with frequent and severe ventricular ectopic rhythms were subjected to psychological stress [13]. The frequency and severity of ventricular ectopic beats increased dramatically during emotional activation of sympathetic mechanisms but not during reflexively-induced increased sympathetic tone.

The hard-wiring of emotion/music and cardiovascular neural systems probably involves many subcortical descending projections from the forebrain and hypothalamus [17–22]. Cardiovascular changes were observed in experiments where the motor cortex surface was stimulated, eliciting tachycardia accompanied by and independent of changes in arterial blood pressure [23]. The 'sigmoid' cortex [23,24], frontal lobe [25–27], especially the medial agranular region [28], subcallosal gyrus [29], septal area [30,31], temporal lobe [32], and cingulate gyrus [32–34] appear to be involved. The insular cortex in cardiac regulation is important because of its high connectivity with the limbic system, suggest-

APPENDIX B *(cont'd)*

Review Article   Med Sci Monit, 2003; 9(5): RA116-121

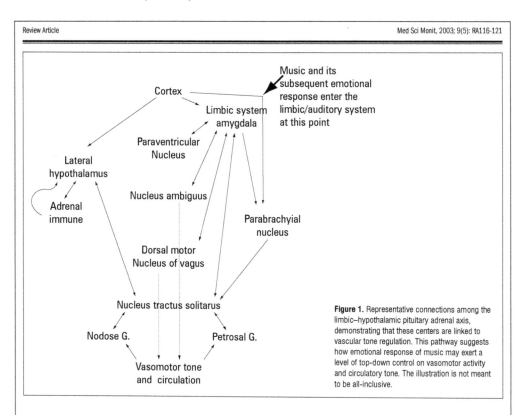

Figure 1. Representative connections among the limbic–hypothalamic pituitary adrenal axis, demonstrating that these centers are linked to vascular tone regulation. This pathway suggests how emotional response of music may exert a level of top-down control on vasomotor activity and circulatory tone. The illustration is not meant to be all-inclusive.

ing that the insula is involved in cardiac rate and rhythm regulation under emotional stress [35–38].

The amygdala, with respect to autonomic-emotional integration [39,40], is composed of numerous subnuclei, which the play a major role in the elaboration of autonomic responses [41]. There are profuse inputs to this region from the insular and orbitofrontal cortices, the parabrachial nucleus, and the nucleus tractus solitarius [42–44]. Amygdalo-tegmental projections are viewed as a critical link in cerebral cortical control of autonomic function [45,46].

The medial hypothalamus is also implicated in cardiac arrhythmogenesis [47]. Beattie and colleagues [47] suggested that hypothalamic projections that descended into the midbrain periaqueductal gray matter, reticular formation, and intermediolateral nucleus of the spinal cord mediate the response. Magoun and colleagues [48] demonstrated that the lateral hypothalamus and wide areas of the lateral tegmentum are also important for autonomic function. The lateral hypothalamus has long been recognized for its role in the regulation of motivation and emotion and the autonomic concomitants of related behaviors [49]. The densest cortical projection to the lateral hypothalamus arises from the infralimbic cortex [50]. Pressor sites within the insular cortex project more heavily to the lateral hypothalamus than do depressor sites and are represented at caudal levels.

Anatomical studies of the lateral hypothalamus demonstrate projections to the periaqueductal gray matter, the parabrachial region, parvicellular formation, dorsal vagal complex, and spinal cord [51,52]. Furthermore, descending projections of the lateral hypothalamus terminate as a capsule around the dorsal motor nucleus of the vagus nerve, which provides secretomotor fibers to the stomach wall, pancreas, and small intestine. These neural patterns might account for the close association of cardiac and gastric responses.

4. NITRIC OXIDE

The very origin of music as a method of stress release has its roots in the early development of the auditory system. In a study by Fessenden and Schacht [53], it was found that the nitric oxide (NO)/cGMP pathway is thoroughly involved in the development and function of the sensory systems, and specifically in the development of the cochlea. Thus NO is involved in the stimulated relaxation from the very development of the organism, to the mechanism by which the relaxation occurs [54]. Cochlear nerve fibers enter the brainstem and are routed through the thalamus to the auditory cortex. It has been demonstrated that it is along this path that the emotion centers within the limbic system are activated (as depicted in Figure 1. the sensation of music enters the diagrammatic neuronal pathway at the limbic system) [55–57]. Furthermore this neuronal pathway from

APPENDIX B *(cont'd)*

Med Sci Monit, 2003; 9(5): RA116-121

Salamon E et al - Sound therapy induced relaxation

auditory nerve to cortex was found to be mediated by NO [58].

When we examine NO signaling, we notice two components the constitutive NO synthase (cNOS) endothelial (e) and neuronal (n) isoforms; see [59]. Constitutive NOS (cNOS), as the name implies, is always expressed. When cNOS is stimulated, NO release occurs for a short period of time, but this level of NO can exert profound physiological actions for a longer period of time [59]. NO is not only an immune, vascular and neural signaling molecule, it is also antibacterial [60,61], antiviral [60,61] and it down-regulates endothelial and immunocyte activation and adherence, thus performing vital physiological activities, including vasodilation [59]. Thus NO release subsequent to music listening, has the potential to protect an organism from microbes and physiologic disorders such as hypertension, and also diminishes excessive immune and endothelial activation occuring largely because of vasodilation modulated by NO [59].

The endocannabinoids, anandamide and 2-arachidonyl glycerol, are naturally occurring cNOS-derived NO-stimulating signaling molecules that are also constitutively expressed [62]. Anandamide, an endogenous endocannabinoid, can also cause NO release from human immune cells, neural tissues and human vascular endothelial cells [63]. Anandamide can also initiate invertebrate immune cell cNOS-derived NO [64]. Estrogen can also stimulate cNOS-derived NO in human immune and vascular cells [63, 65]. We believe that each signaling system performs this common function under different circumstances. Morphine, another naturally occurring animal signal molecule [66], given its long latency before increases in its levels are detected, arises after trauma/inflammation and, through a NO mechanism, down regulates these processes in neural and immune tissues [67]. Anandamide, as part of the ubiquitous arachidonate and eicosanoid signaling cascade, serves to maintain and augment tonal NO in vascular tissues [59]. Estrogen, through NO release, provides an additional pathway by which the system can down-regulate immunocyte and vascular function in women [63]. This may be due to both the immune and vascular trauma associated with cyclic reproductive activities, such as endometrial buildup, when a high degree of vascular and immune activities are occurring. Given the extent of proliferative growth capacity during peak estrogen levels in this cycle, NO may function to enhance down-regulation of the immune system to allow for these changes. Clearly, therefore, enhanced cNOS activity would be a beneficial effect within the concept and time framework of music and the subsequent relaxation it induces. Thus, these signal molecules, especially endocannabinoid and opiate alkaloids [68] have the potential to make you 'feel' good and relax [69], also release NO, which may be a vital part of this complicated process.

5. SIGNALING MOLECULES LEADING TO RELAXATION

As noted above, once individuals undergo a very mild form of work/activity such as music listening, they experience peripheral vasodilation, warming of the skin, a decrease in heart rate and an overwhelming sense of well-being [7,69].

In examining a potential mechanism for the music induced relaxation, besides the over-riding central nervous system output via the autonomic nervous system, peripheral neuro-vascular processes would appear to be important. We surmise NO to be of fundamental importance in this response because of the increase in peripheral temperature, i.e, vasodilation [70]. For a complete review of possible related mechanisms see [59,71–73].

We also surmise, based on current studies, that endothelial derived NO, released through normal pulsations, due to vascular dynamics responding to heart beat [59] as well as ACh stimulated endothelial NO release, may contribute to the effect of NO in inducing smooth muscle relaxation [74]. Furthermore, vascular pulsations may be of sufficient strength to also stimulate nNOS derived NO release, limiting any basal NE actions [74]. Interestingly, nitrosative stress, mediated by involvement of the reactive nitrogen oxide species, N2O3 does inhibit dopamine hydroxylase, inhibiting NE synthesis and contributing to the regulation of neurotransmission and vasodilation [75].This system may provide an autoregulatory mechanism involved in the neuronal control of peripheral vasomotor responses.

6. CONCLUSION

In summary, the music induced relaxation peripherally appears to be mediated by a system of regulation involving NO, as neurotransmitter and as a locally acting hormone. Contingent on the preliminary vasoconstriction and depolarization of the membrane, vasodilation is mediated by NO liberated from vasodilator nerves that activate guanylate cyclase in smooth muscle and produce cGMP. During this stage, NO and NE exist simultaneously. Due to the characteristics of NO, NE no longer mediates vasoconstriction; instead NO activates guanylate cyclase, which produces vasodilation and the relaxation under a depolarized membrane state (see [30,54,76]).

In conclusion, the above findings demonstrate that music has numerous profound effects [4–6,68, see also [77] for social effects] we believe that this occurs via NO, opiate and the above mentioned hormonal system. Furthermore NO has been shown to be a necessary molecule in the development of the auditory system [53], which is required to enable music to act as a relaxant. Taken together we believe that the complex nitric oxide signaling system is the primary and fundamental (from development to mechanism) method by which music acts as a relaxation device.

APPENDIX B *(cont'd)*

Review Article

Med Sci Monit, 2003; 9(5): RA116-121

REFERENCES:

1. McEwen BS: Protective and damaging effects of stress mediation. New Engl J Med, 1998; 338: 171-179

2. Chrousos GP, Gold PW: The concepts of stress and stress system disorders: Overview of physical and behavioral homeostasis. J Am Med Assoc, 1992; 267

3. Fricchione GL, Stefano GB: The stress response and autoimmunoregulation. Adv Neuroimmunol, 1994; 4: 13-28.

4. Tusek DL, Church JM, Strong SA et a: Guided Imagery A Significant Advance in the Care of Patients Undergoing Elective Colorectal Surgery. Diseases of the Colon and Rectum, 1996; 40: 172-178

5. Aldridge K: The Use of Music to Relieve Pre-operational Anxiety in Children Attending Day Surgery. The Australian Journal of Music Therapy, 1993; 4: 19-35

6. Mullooly VM, Levin RF, Feldman HR: Music for Postoperative Pain and Anxiety. Journal of New York State Nurses Association, 1988; 19: 4-7

7. Steelman V: M Intraoperative Music Therapy Effects on Anxiety, Blood Pressure. AORN Journal, 1990; 52: 1026-1034

8. Schuster B: LThe Effect of Music Listening on Blood Pressure Fluctuations in Adult Hemeodialysis Patients. Journal of Music Therapy, 3: 146-153

9. Zimmerman LM, Pierson MA, Marker J: 1988. Effects of Music on Patient Anxiety in Coronary Care Units. Heart and Lung, 1985; 17: 560-566

10. Damasio AR: Descartes' Error: Emotion, Reason, and the Human Brain, Putnam, New York, 1994

11. Stefano GB, Fricchione GL: The biology of deception: Emotion and morphine. Med Hypotheses 49, 1995; 51-54

12. Stefano GB, Fricchione GL: The biology of deception: The evolution of cognitive coping as a denial-like process. Med, . Hypotheses, 1995; 44: 311-314

13. Lown B, DeSilva RA: Roles of psychologic stress and autonomic nervous system changes in provocation of ventricular premature complexes. Am J Cardiol, 1978; 41: 979-985

14. Lown B, Verrier RL: Neural activity and ventricular fibrillation. New Engl J Med, 1976; 294: 1165-1170

15. Wellens HJ, Vermeulen A, Durrer D; Ventricular fibrillation occurring on arousal from sleep by auditory stimuli. Circulation, 1972; 46: 661-665

16. Schiffer F, Hartley LH, Schulman CL, Abelmann WH: Evidence for emotionally-induced coronary arterial spasm in patients with angina pectoris. Br Heart J, 1980; 44: 62-66

17. Holstege G: Some anatomical observations on the projections from the hypothalamus to brainstem and spinal cord: an HRP and autoradiographic tracing study in the cat. J Comp Neurol, 1987; 260: 98-126

18. Holstege G, Meiners L, Tan K: Projections of the bed nucleus of the stria terminalis to the mesencephalon, pons, and medulla oblongata in the cat. Exp Brain Res, 1985; 58: 379-391

19. Hopkins DA: Amygdalotegmentalprojections in the rat, cat and rhesus monkey. Neurosci Lett, 1975; 1: 263-270

20. Hopkins DA, Holstege G: Amygdaloid projections to the mesencephalon, pons and medulla oblongata in the cat. Exp Brain Res, 1978; 32: 529-547

21. Kuypers HGJM, Maisky VA: Retrograde axonal transport of horseradish peroxidase from spinal cord to brainstem cell groups in the cat. Neurosci Lett, 1975; 1: 9-14

22. Swanson LW, Kuypers HG: The paraventricular nucleus of the hypothalamus: cytoarchitectonic subdivisions and organization of projections to the pituitary, dorsal vagal complex, and spinal cord as demonstrated by retrograde fluorescence double-labeling methods. J Comp Neurol, 1980; 194: 555-570

23. Schiff M: Untersuchungen ueber die motorischen Functionen des Grosshirns. Arch Exp Pathol Pharmakol Naunyn Schmiedeberg, 1875; 3: 171-179

24. Cerevkov A: Ueber den einfluss der Gehirnhemisphaeren auf das Herz und auf das Gefassystem, Guseff, Kharkov, Russia, 1892

25. Crouch RL, Thompson JK: Autonomic functions of the cerebral cortex. J Nerv Ment Dis, 1939; 89: 328-334

26. Hsu S, Hwang K, Chu H: A study of the cardiovascular changes induced by stimulation of the motor cortex in dogs. Am J Physiol, 1942; 137: 468-472

27. Winkler C: Attention and respiration. Proc Acad Sci Amsterdam, 1899; 1: 121-138

28. Buchanan SL, Valentine J, Powell DA: Autonomic responses are elicited by electrical stimulation of the medial but not lateral frontal cortex in rabbits. Behav Brain Res, 1985; 18: 51-62

29. Hoff EC: The role of the cerebral cortex in the central nervous regulation of cardiovascular function. Confin Neurol, 1949; 9: 166-176

30. de la Torre JC, Stefano GB: Evidence that Alzheimer's disease is a microvascular disorder: The role of constituitive nitric oxide. Brain Res Rev, 2000; 11: 1581-1585

31. Deutsch DG, Goligorsky MS, Stefano GB et al: Production and physiological actions of anandamide in the vasculature of the rat kidney. J Clin Invest, 1997; 100: 1538-1546

32. MacLean PD: Discussion. Physiol Rev, 1960; 40: 113-114

33. Smith WK: The functional significance of the rostral cingular cortex as revealed by its responses to electrical excitation. J Neurophysiol, 1945; 8: 241-254

34. Ueda H: Arrhythmias produced by cerebral stimulation. Jpn Circ J, 1962; 26: 225-230

35. Fimiani C, Liberty T, Aquirre AJ et al: Opiate, cannabinoid, and eicosanoid signaling converges on common intracellular pathways: Nitric oxide coupling. Prostaglandins, 1998; 57: 23-34

36. Russchen FT: Amygdalopetal projections in the cat. I. Cortical afferent connections. A study with retrograde and anterograde tracing techniques. J Comp Neurol, 1982; 206: 159-179

37. Calaresu FR, Ciriello J: Projections to the hypothalamus from buffer nerves and nucleus tractus solitarius in the cat. Am J Physiol, 1980; 239: 130-136

38. Melville KI, Blum G, Shister HE, Silver MD: Cardiac ischemic changes and arrhythmias induced by hypothalamic stimulation. Am J Cardiol, 1963; 12: 781-791

39. Davis M: The role of the amygdala in fear and anxiety. Annu Rev Neurosci, 1992; 15: 353-375

40. Kapp BS, Frysinger RC, Gallagher M, Haselton JR: Amygdala central nucleus lesions: effect on heart rate conditioning in the rabbit. Physiol. Behav, 1979; 23: 1109-1117

41. Mansson E, Bare LA, Yang D: Isolation of a human kappa opioid receptor cDNA from placenta. Biochem Biophys Res Commun, 1994; 202: 1431

42. Yasui Y, Itoh K, Kaneko T: Topographical projections from the cerebral cortex to the nucleus of the solitary tract in the cat. Exp Brain Res, 1991; 85: 75-84

43. Friedman R, Zuttermeister P, Benson H: Letter to the editor. New Engl J Med, 1993; 329: 1201

44. Bonvallet M, Bobo EG: Changes in phrenic activity and heart rate elicited by localized stimulation of amygdala and adjacent structures. Electroencephalogr. Clin Neurophysiol, 1972; 32: 1-16

45. Allen GV, Saper CB, Hurley KM, Cechetto DF: Organization of visceral and limbic connections in the insular cortex of the rat. J Comp Neurol, 1991; 311: 1-16

46. Kapp BS, Schwaber JS, Driscoll PA: Frontal cortex projections to the amygdaloid central nucleus in the rabbit. Neuroscience, 1985; 15: 327-346

47. Beattie J, Brow GR, Long CNH: Physiological and anatomical evidence for the existence of nerve tracts connecting the hypothalamus with spinal sympathetic centres. Proc R Soc Lond B, 1930; 106: 253-275

48. Magoun HW, Ranson SW, Heatherington A: Descending connections from the hypothalamus. Arch Neurol Psychiatry, 1938; 39: 1127-1149

49. Saper CB, Swanson LW, Cowan WM: An autoradiographic study of the efferent connections of the lateral hypothalamic area in the rat. J Comp Neurol, 1979; 183: 689-706

50. Hurley KM, Herbert H, Moga MM, Saper CB: Efferent projections of the infralimbic cortex of the rat. J Comp Neurol, 1991; 308: 249-276

51. Hosoya Y, Matsushita M: Brainstem projections from the lateral hypothalamic area in the rat, as studied with autoradiography. Neurosci Lett, 1981; 24: 111-116

APPENDIX B *(cont'd)*

Med Sci Monit, 2003; 9(5): RA116-121 Salamon E et al - Sound therapy induced relaxation

52. ter Horst GJ, Luiten PG, Kuipers F: Descending pathways from hypothalamus to dorsal motor vagus and ambiguus nuclei in the rat. J Auton Nerv Syst, 1984; 11: 59-75

53. Fessenden JD, Schacht J: The nitric oxide/cyclic GMP pathway: a potential major regulator of cochlear physiology. Hearing Research, 1998; 118(1-2): 168-176

54. Stefano GB, Goumon Y, Bilfinger TV et al: Basal nitric oxide limits immune, nervous and cardiovascular excitation: Human endothelia express a mu opiate receptor. Prog Neurobiol, 2000; 60: 531-544

55. Blood AJ, Zatorre RJ: Intensely pleasurable responses to music correlate with activity in brain regions implicated in reward and emotion. Proc Natl Acad Sci, 2001; 25; 98(20): 11818-23

56. Blood AJ, Zatorre RJ, Bermudez P, Evans AC: Emotional responses to pleasant and unpleasant music correlate with activity in paralimbic brain regions. Nat Neurosci, 1999; 2(4): 382-7

57. Zatorre RJ, Evans AC, Meyer E: Neural mechanisms underlying melodic perception and memory for pitch. J Neurosci, 1994; 14(4): 1908-19

58. Michel O, Hess A, Bloch W et al: Localization of the NO/cGMP-pathway in the cochlea of guinea pigs. Hear Res, 1999; 133(1-2): 1-9

59. Chung JW, Schacht J: ATP and nitric oxide modulate intracellular calcium in isolated pillar cells of the guinea pig cochlea. J Assoc Res Otolaryngol, 2001; 2(4): 399-407

60. Benz D, Cadet P, Mantione K et al: (2002) Tonal nitric oxide and health: A free radical and a scavenger of free radicals. Med Sci, Monitor, 2002; 8: 1-4

61. Benz D, Cadet P, Mantione K et al: Tonal nitric oxide and health: Anti-Bacterial and –Viral Actions and Implications for HIV. Med Sci Monitor, 2002; 8(1): 27-31

62. Stefano GB, Salzet M, Magazine HI: Bilfinger, Antagonism of LPS and IFN-Błąd! Nieznany argument przełącznika. induction of iNOS in human saphenous vein endothelium by morphine and anandamide by nitric oxide inhibition of adenylate cyclase. J Cardiovasc, Pharmacol, 1998: 31: 813-820

63. Stefano GB, Salzet M: Bilfinger, Long-term exposure of human blood vessels to HIV gp120, morphine and anandamide increases endothelial adhesion of monocytes: Uncoupling of nitric oxide. J Cardiovasc Pharmacol, 1998; 31: 862-868

64. Stefano GB, Salzet B, Salzet M: Identification and characterization of the leech CNS cannabinoid receptor: Coupling to nitric oxide release. Brain Res, 1997; 753: 219-224

65. Stefano GB, Cadet P, Breton C et al: Estradiol-stimulated nitric oxide release in human granulocytes is dependent on intracellular calcium transients: Evidence for a cell surface estrogen receptor. Blood, 2000; 95: 3951-3958

66. Stefano GB, Goumon Y, Casares F et al: Endogenous morphine. Trends Neurosci, 2000; 9: 436-442

66. Lembo G, Vecchione C, Izzo R et al: Noradrenergic vascular hyper-responsiveness in human hypertension is dependent on oxygen free radical impairment of nitric oxide activity. Circulation, 2000; 102: 552-557

67. Tonnesen E, Brix-Christensen V, Bilfinger TV et al: Endogenous morphine levels increase following cardiac surgery: Decreasing proinflammatory cytokine levels and immunocyte activity. Int J Cardiol, 1998; 62; 191-197

68. Snyder M, Chlan L: Music Therapy. Annu Rev Nurs Res, 1999; 17: 3-25

69. Krumhansl CL: An exploratory study of musical emotions and psychophysiology Can J Exp Psychol, 1997; 51(4): 336-53

70. Stuart EM, Caudill J, Leserman C et al: Nonpharmacologic treatment of hypertension: A multiple-risk-factor approach. J Cardiovasc Nurs, 1987; 1: 1-14

71. Okamura T, Ayajiki K, Uchiyama M et al: Neurogenic vasodilatation of canine isolated small labial arteries. J. Pharmacol. Exp Ther, 1999; 288: 1031-1036

72. Toda N: Mediation by nitric oxide of neurally-induced human cerebral artery relaxation. Experientia, 1993; 49 51-53

APPENDIX C

BioSonic Repatterning™

BioSonic Repatterning is an energy medicine approach to sound therapy developed by Dr. John Beaulieu. BioSonic means LifeSound. BioSonic Repatterning is the process of tuning into and aligning the rhythms inherent in nature with our LifeSound. BioSonic Repatterning is based on an understanding of life as vibrational in nature. The fundamental organizing and sustaining factor of our being is Sound, with a capital S. Our LifeSound, like a vibrating string, divides again and again to create harmonics. The natural rhythms of our body are harmonics of our LifeSound. By tuning into and listening to our body rhythms, i.e., respiratory rhythms, craniosacral rhythms, cardiac rhythms, and organ rhythms, we can access their source in a similar way a dancer moves through different musical rhythms to their underlying beat.

The journey from harmonic rhythms to our LifeSound is a process of unwinding through different vibrational states. These states manifest to the practitioner as a series of images, thoughts, emotions, postures, movement patterns, tissue responses, and physical sensations. The guiding principle is a felt body sense of resonance, stillness, and dissonance. As long as the practitioner stays centered and open, the result will be a resonate connection between harmonics and LifeSound.

An important area of BioSonic Repatterning is understanding our physical structure via our skeletal system as a harmonic extension of our LifeSound. A bodywork practitioner can use this knowledge as a map to align body areas to visual harmonic patterns. The process of physical harmonic alignment often creates a resonance throughout the self which leads to deeper levels of sonic unwinding and greater rhythmic alignment. This can further be facilitated by BioSonic tuning forks tuned to Pythagorean intervals in alignment with skeletal harmonic proportions.

BioSonic Repatterning integrates into the practitioner's method of working. For example, a massage practitioner may create different rhythmic strokes based on BioSonic evaluation combined with muscle-skeletal evaluation. A cranial practitioner may gently follow the cranial rhythm into different harmonic levels, and an energy practitioner may use spinal stretch releases and connective tissue strokes to align a body to natural harmonic patterns. In addition, practitioners trained in

BioSonic Repatterning may use specific modalities which include tuning forks, music, color and light, precious stones, toning, mantras, chanting, voice, music improvisation, and rhythmic movement to create a resonance with one's Life-Sound.

In relationship to verbal communication skills, BioSonic Repatterning integrates voice rhythms, speed, pitch, and volume; emotional rhythms; and general movement patterns between people. A bodywork practitioner or psychotherapist may use these skills to gain rapport with a client, evaluate a client, or intervene to match rhythms between different areas of a clients verbal expression. Practitioners integrating BioSonic Reapatterning voice and listening skills report a new dimension to their work that enhances both verbal and non verbal communication leading to an increased sense of well-being.

BioSonic Repatterning was discovered and developed by John Beaulieu, N.D., Ph.D. Beginning in the early 1970's. Dr. Beaulieu sat in an anechoic chamber, a completely silent and dark room, for over five hundred hours over a period of two years listening to the sounds of his body. Being a music therapist and composer, he began to notice different sound, rhythmic, and intervalic phenomena within his body which led him to healings in his own life. These experiences became guides in developing the new music and sound therapy processes and technologies that he terms BioSonic Repatterning.

BioSonic Repatterning training programs are available on dvd and in class with Dr. Beaulieu. For more information visit www.BioSonics.com.

APPENDIX D

BioSonic Tuning Fork Manufacturing Standards

The tuning forks displayed in Human Tuning are manufactured by BioSonic Enterprises, Ltd. BioSonic tuning forks are designed to scientific standards using the highest quality aluminum alloy. They are precisely tuned within 0.5% of the indicated frequency at 20° C. All tuning forks are subjected to at least three inspection processes to guarantee quality. The specially designed aluminum alloy makes them harder, more durable, and impact resistant with decreased frequency changes due to temperature variations. This results in a longer ring tone, purer tonal quality when knee tapped, and a complete range of overtones when tapped together. Using the highest quality aluminum alloy also means that Bio-Sonic tuning forks are immune to corrosion, have the highest rating for quality of surface finish, and have no sharp edges.

BioSonic tuning forks are made with Alcoa aluminum. The aluminum is domestically produced within the regulations of United States and meets all environmental laws. Alcoa was named one of the top three Sustainable Corporations in the World Economic Forum in Davos, Switzerland. In 2005, Business Week magazine, in conjunction with the Climate Group, ranked Alcoa as one of the "Top Green Companies" in cutting their carbon gas emissions.

Aluminum tuning forks tested from other companies are softer, have higher levels of impurities, and are more susceptible to corrosion and frequency changes due to temperature variations. They have a rougher appearance, the ring time is 20+% less, and tonal quality, which is important in the healing process, can vary by 2+%. Due to the softness of the aluminum many overtones, which are essential in neural transmission as part of stress reduction are dropped and cannot be relied upon with any consistency. The companies supplying the softer impure aluminum tuning forks tend to have weak environment records and questionable labor practices.

BIBLIOGRAPHY

———■———

Arroyo, Stephan. *Astrology, Psychology, and the Four Elements*. Reno, NV: CRCS Press, 1975.

Ashton, Anthony. *Harmonograph: A Visual Guide to the Mathematics of Music*. New York, NY: Walker and Company, 2003.

Beaulieu, J. *Music and Sound in the Healing Arts*. Barrytown, NY: Station Hill Press, 1987.

Beaulieu, J. *Polarity Therapy Workbook*. New York, NY: BioSonic Enterprises, 1994.

Becker, Rollin E. *Life in Motion*. Portland, OR: Rudra Press, 1997.

Benson, H., W. Proctor *The Break-Out Principle*. New York, NY: Scribner, 2003.

Bertalanffy, Ludwig von. *General System Theory: Foundations, Development, Applications*. New York, NY: George Braziller, 1968.

Bomberger, C., & J. Haar. "Effects of sound stress on the migration of prethymic stem cells." *Annals of the New York Academy of Sciences*, 1988: 540, 700-701.

Cage, John. *Silence*. Middletown, NY: Wesleyan University Press, 1965.

Castaneda, Carlos. *The Teachings of Don Juan: A Yaqui Way of Knowledge*. New York, NY: Simon & Schuster, 1968.

Cooke, J.P. *The Cardiovascular Cure*. New York, NY: Broadway Books, 2002.

Cousto, Hans. *The Cosmic Octave: Origin of Harmony*. Mendocino, CA: Life Rhythm, 1988.

Coxhead, D., and S. Hiller. *Dreams*. New York, NY: Crossroad Publishing Company, 1976.

Dahl, M., E. Rice, & D. Groesbeck. "Effects of fiber motion on the acoustic behavior of an anistropic flexible fibrous membrane." *Journal of the Acoustical Society of America*, 1990: 87, 416-422.

Doczi, Gyorgy. *The Power of Limits: Proportional Harmonies in Nature, Art, & Architecture.* Boston, MA: New Science Library, 1982.

Earlewine, Mitch. *Understanding Marijuana.* England: Oxford University Press, 2002.

Epstein, R.H. "Puff the Magic Gas." Physician's Weekly online: August 19, 1996.

Fountain, H. "Discovering the Tricks of Fireflies: Summertime Magic." *New York Times,* July 3, 2001, D4.

Garland, Trudi, C. Kahn. *Math and Music: Harmonious Connections.* Parsippany, NJ: Dale Seymour Publications, 1995.

Gendlin, Eugene. *Let Your Body Interpret Your Dreams.* Wilmette, IL: Chiron Publications, 1986.

Goldman, J. *Healing Sounds: The Power of Harmonics.* Rockport, MA: Element Books, 1992.

Hall, Manly P. *The Therapeutic Value of Music.* Los Angeles, CA: The Philosophical Research Society, 1955.

Henry, J.L. "Circulating opioids: possible physiological roles in central nervous function." *Neuroscience and Biobehavioral Review 6,* 1982.

Jeans, James. *Science and Music.* New York, NY: Dover Publications, 1987.

Jenny, Hans. *Cymatics: The Structure and Dynamics of Waves and Vibrations.* Basel, Switzerland: Basilius Presse, 1974.

Khan, Hazrat Inayat. *Music.* New York, NY: Samuel Weiser, 1962.

Knanna, Madhu. *Yantra: The Tantric Symbol of Cosmic Unity.* England: Thames and Hudson, 1979.

Klossowski, R. *Alchemy: The Secret Art.* New York, NY: Thames and Hudson Inc, 1973.

Lauterwasser, A. *Water Sound Images: The Creative Music of the Universe.* Newmarket, NH: Macromedia Publishing, 2002.

Lincoln, Jill, C. Hoyle, and G. Burnstock. *Nitric Oxide in Health and Disease.* England: Cambridge University Press, 1997.

Lenhardt, M., R. Skellett, and P. Wang. "Human ultrasonic speech perception." *Science,* 1991: 253, 82-85.

Livio, Mario. *The Golden Ratio.* New York, NY: Broadway Books, 1992.

Magoun, Harold I. *Osteopathy in the Cranial Field.* Kirksville, MO: Journal Printing, 1976.

Metzner, Ralph. *Human Consciousness and the Spirits of Nature*. New York, NY: Thunders Mouth Press, 1999.

Mookerjee, A. *Kundalini: The Arousal of the Inner Energy*. Rochester, VT: Destiny Books, 1991.

Ouspensky, P. D. *In Search of the Miraculous*. New York, NY: Harvest Books, 1949.

Petsch, H. "Approaches to verbal, visual, and musical creativity by EEG coherence analysis." *International Journal of Psychophysiology 24,* 1996.

Rael, Joseph. *Being and Vibration*. Tulsa, OK: Council Oak Books, 1993.

Rudhyar, Dane. *The Magic of Tone and the Art of Music*. Boulder, CO: Shambhala, 1982.

Schneider, M. *A Beginner's Guide to Constructing the Universe: The Mathematical Archetypes of Nature, Art, and Science,*. New York, NY: Harper Collins, 1994.

Scott, Cyrill. *Music: Its Secret Influence Through the Ages*. London: Theosophical Publishing House, 1937.

Schwenk, Theodor. *Sensitive Chaos: The Creation of Flowing Forms in Water & Air*. New York, NY: Schocken Books, 1976.

Stefano, G. B., G. L. Fricchione, B. T. Slingsby, H. Benson. "The Placebo Effect and the Relaxation Response: Neural Processes and their Coupling to Constitutive Nitric Oxide." *Brain Research Reviews 35*, 2001.

Stefano, G. B., Salzet, M. "Invertebrate opioid precursors: evolutionary conversation and the significance of enzymatic processing." *Int Rev Cytol*, 1999.

Stone, R. *Polarity Therapy: The Complete Works. Vol I*. Reno, NV: CRCS Publications, 1987.

Stone, R. *Polarity Therapy: The Complete Works. Vol II*. Reno, NV: CRCS Publications, 1987.

Strassman, Rick. *DMT: The Spirit Molecule*. Vermont: Park Street Press, 2001.

Sutherland, W. G. *Contributions to Thought*. Fort Worth, TX: Rudra Press, 1967.

Tansley, David. *Subtle Body*. New York, NY: Thames and Hudson, 1985.

Upledger, J., and J. Vredevoogd. *Craniosacral Therapy: Vol I*. Seattle, WA: Eastland Press, 1983.

Urazaev, A. K., A. L. Zefirov. "The physiological role of nitric oxide." *Uspekhi Fiziologicheskikh Nauk*, 1999.

Wieder, June. *Song of the Spine*. Brookridge, SC: Booksurge Publishing, 2004.

ACKNOWLEDGEMENTS

———■———

There are many people who have helped me to complete *Human Tuning*.

First and foremost I want to thank all my students for being there and asking lots of questions.

My Mother and Father for gave me everything I needed to be myself.

My wife Thea Keats Beaulieu and my twin sons Daniel and Lukas Beaulieu, the intervals of my life.

My son Lars Beaulieu and my granddaughter Lua Beaulieu, the overtones of my life.

Pamela Kersage for her years of support and always being there.

Jackson MacLow who brought poetry to everything he touched.

Sathya Sai Baba for spiritual guidance.

Franz Kamin for musical guidance.

Sofia Rosoff for the authentic rhythm within the rhythm.

William R. Howell, Esq., for opening up a new vista where both science and energy can be integrated.

Scott Jefferies and Zak and Jacob Smith for all their support and bringing BioSonics into the 21st century.

Georgio and Camille Palmisano for all their love and support.

The Cell Dynamics Research Team: George B. Stefano, Elliott Salamon, and Minsun Kim for their scientific dedication and willingness to work with sound.

Peter and Julie Wetzler for their living art and inspiring everyone around them to be creative.

Bob and Mary Swanson, of Riverbank Laboratories, Inc., who keep us tuned.

Gerry and Barbara Hand Clow for their friendship, vision, and energy counsel.

Philippe Garnier (Sage Center, Woodstock, NY) who gave us a visionary book cover.

Gary Strauss and Tracy Griffiths (Polarity Healing Arts Los Angeles California) for their support and creating a healing center which represents the essence of Polarity Therapy.

Andreas and Brigitta Raiman Lederman (Schule fur Holistische Naturheilkunde Zug, Switzerland) for their many years of friendship and support.

Urs and Paki Hanauer (Polarity Zentrum, Zurich, Switzerland) for their many years of friendship and support.

Rex and Alaea Beynon (Brynoch Farm) Wales for many years of support and friendship.

Jeff Volk of Macromedia for his many years of support and sound discussions.

Jonathan and Andi Goldman who vibrate like tuning forks in the sound healing world and have always encouraged and supported my work.

George Quasha and Charles Stein for their years of support and inspiring conversations.

Frank and Judy Rubin Bosco, David and Lisa Sokoloff Gonzalez, Music Therapists who represent the essence of music healing.

Vicki Genfann who sings and sounds for all to hear.

Swami Srinivasan, Swami Swaroopananda, and the all the staff of the Sivananda Yoga Centers for their spiritual support, vision, and great Carribean conversations.

Silvia Nakkach and Michael Knapp (Vox Mundi Berkley, California) for sharing their love of music and sound and inspiring all around them.

Ueli Gasser and Peter Wiedler for sharing their knowledge of energy, alchemy, music, and healing over many years.

David Holtz and Tim Leach (SomaEnergetics) for their support and work with sound.

Catherine Vitte for her support, kindness, and great talks about sound and the cranium.

Zacciah Blackburn (New England Sound Healers) for believing in the sound healing and bringing it into the world.

Phillip Young (Polarity Network) for sharing his vision of Polarity Therapy.

Isa Dollyhigh, R.P.P., who sang the essence of sound healing.

John Cage who sat so still and showed me the silence within the sound.

Innas Xenakis whose formalized music lead me into the infinite mathematics of sound.

Karen Krane (High Vibes Distribution) for her support and feedback on many projects.

Michael Kopel for his special insights and dedication.

CPSIA information can be obtained
at www.ICGtesting.com
Printed in the USA
BVHW052337310821
615076BV00015B/2

9 780615 358857